SHORTCUTS
to POLAND

2nd edition

For Kath'—the Fin, my friend

About the author:

After earning a master's degree from Georgetown University, Laura Klos Sokol came to Poland on a Fulbright lectureship in 1992 and taught at the University of Warsaw. She planned to stay for one year. She now works as a freelance corporate trainer in Warsaw. She and her Polish husband have a daughter and are settled permanently in Poland.

The Author's Dog

SHORTCUTS
to POLAND

2nd edition

LAURA
KLOS SOKOL

Warszawa, 2005

Copyright © 2004 by IPS

2nd edition: 2005

Published by: International Publishing Service Sp. z o.o.

Most of the material in this book originally appeared, in a slightly different form, in The Warsaw Voice: Polish and Central European Review. The article, *Starting to Get It,* originally appeared in Polish in the magazine Charaktery.

Cover and illustration design by: Piotr Ziółkowski

Copy Editors: Steve Owad with Nate Espino

Typesetting: P.W. LESPOL S.c.

ISBN 83-921149-0-6

Contents

INTRODUCTION 7

The First Step 9
   The Polskość Quiz 9

Some Behaviors 12
   Enigmatic Ice Breakers 12
   The #1 Question 15
   Seeking Therapeutic Friendship 18
   Breezy Easy 20
   The Big But 23
   Scoring Help 26
   Summons on the Rebound 29
   Proper Chowing Down 32
   Stuffing Yourself Silly 34
   A Host of Talk 37
   Public Love 40
   An Advice Column 44
   Public Heat 47
   Verbal Strokes 50
   Shhhhhhh! 52
   Unbridled Hilarity 55
   Honest Cheating 57
   A Fireside Chat about Money 59
   Tips for the Unruly 61
   In Tune with Tone 64
   Mammal Message 67
   Smile Code 69
   Socially Behind 72
   One Touchy Subject 74
   A National Priority 76
   Phoney Behavior 78

Your Work Life 81
   New Poles and Ambition 81
   Workplace Families 84
   The Schmooze Department 87
   A Terribly Good Job 89
   The Buck Stops Here...or There 92
   Sweaty Salesmanship 95
   Work vs. Real Life 98

Polish Specifics 100
- The Age Box 100
- Family Ties 103
- Meet the Cast 107
- Tongueless Talk 109
- Saint Garlic 112
- Name of the Day 114
- Your Lucky Day 116
- Blooming Protocol 119
- Christmas Spirit, Slavic Soul 121
- The Weirdest Christmas Ever 123

Other Curiosities 127
- One Hell of a Romantic Trip 127
- Lip Action 130
- Manners 101 132
- Expat Culture 134
- Reality Check 136
- Bureaucracy Fun and Games 138
- Ethno-types in Stereo 141

A Language Booster 143
- Six and Violins 143
- A Rootin' Tootin' Good Time 145
- The Ritual of Liquid Charm 148
- Thanksaroonie 151
- The Tune of Bye 154
- Pan, Pani, or Hey You? 157
- Dubbing Rights 160
- The Polglish Language 162
- Favorite False Friends 164
- Crash! Bam! Pow! 166
- When Slang Don't Clang 168
- P is for Prefix 170
- Accent on Charm 172
- Starting to Get It 174

Your Final Task 180
- The American Quiz 180

INTRODUCTION

When I meet Poles for the first time, they're surprised to hear that as an American, I have settled permanently in Poland, and they often want to know why. It's an interesting country, I say, I like the lifestyle and the people. Some are genuinely pleased; others think I'm some kind of weirdo. Some challenge me and point out troubles with the economy, corrupt politicians and the tax system. Gee, it all sounds pretty normal to me—what country in the world is exempt from those types of problems?

Poles are quick to criticize their own country, but don't be fooled: Their national pride is fierce. Besides, it's easy to focus on the problems in Poland; don't let them overshadow the achievements of the last 15 years or so. If you haven't been in Poland for long, the strides in economic and social progress might escape you. But the process of revising this book, updating (and often discarding) texts first written ten years ago, has made me aware yet again of how fast things are changing.

Poles' entrepreneurial spirit is impressive, and though we've come to take it for granted, EU membership is an amazing accomplishment. The effects won't be obvious for a few years, but it's certainly a psychological boost for the country—especially among younger generations.

Now here comes the obligatory disclaimer that I hope is obvious: Not every Pole and American behave in the ways I've described. I see great differences between how younger and older Poles behave, and have tried to point out which behaviors seem to be in flux. And if you're a foreigner working in a multinational, you might be experiencing a different Poland than I describe here.

Sometimes the best I could do was to write about the existing rules and norms of cultural behaviors, not about the exceptions. That means I've resorted to making some generalizations—but I see no way to write about culture other than by freezing reality for a moment. And besides, I think that we sometimes have to speak in generalizations about human behavior, because if we didn't, we wouldn't speak about it at all.

And although the essays on cross-cultural communications are mostly directed at Americans, I hope they'll offer at least some help to other foreigners trying to find their way through Poland.

I want to thank Steve Owad for his rockin' editing skills—nearly everything that I have written over the years has passed under his big nose. While he was ice-fishing, Nate Espino filled in and he's a damn good editor too. Of course, any mistakes are my fault. A big thanks to Beata Taras for keeping things together, to Tom and Lotta Keller for their occasional hounding to do this second edition, and to Janusz, Michał, Łukasz, and especially Tomek at Kawiarnia Lokalna. I'm most grateful to my home treasures, Marek and Olivia, for their patient support.

The First Step

◎ The Polskość Quiz

How Polish are you? Just a tad? Or even more Polish than the Poles? Take this quiz and discover your rate of Polishness:

1. In the past three months, have you spent over three hours sitting at a table. eating and drinking? 3 points for yes; 0 for no.

2. Do you like Prince Polo or Ptasie Mleczko? 3 points for yes; 0 for no; -1 if you don't know what either one is.

3. Have you ever bought shampoo or toothpaste at a kiosk? 2 points for yes; 0 for no; -2 if you've never bought anything at a kiosk.

4. When you are a guest at someone's home for the first time, would you most likely show up with flowers or a gift of some kind? 3 points for yes; -1 for no.

5. Do you normally shake hands with (or kiss) everyone rather than wave hello or good-bye to the group? 3 points for yes; 0 for no.

6. Have you eaten herring? Smoked eel? Carp? 1 point for each fish; add 1 point for each one you enjoy; -2 if you've never eaten any of them.

7. Have you ever had a family member visit for longer than two weeks? 2 points for yes; 0 for no.

8. Have you slept regularly on a convertible or a pull-out bed? 4 points for yes; add 2 points if you fold it up every day; 0 for no; -1 if there isn't such a bed in your home.

9. Does your last name have three syllables or more or at least a 3:1 ratio of consonant to vowel? 1 point for yes; 0 for no.

10. When you're at the table with friends, does someone usually give a toast at some point in the evening? 3 points for yes; 0 for no.

11. Have you strolled through Łazienki Park on a Sunday afternoon? 3 points for yes; add 3 points if you were dressed nicely; 0 for no; -1 if you don't know where the park is or have never been.

12. Do you go to church on most holidays? 2 points for yes; 0 for no.

13. Do you hold strong views on what *bigos* should taste like? 2 points for yes; 0 for no; -1 if you've never had it homemade.

14. When guests arrive at your home, do you immediately offer them something to drink? 2 points for yes; 0 for no.

15. Have you ever entertained twelve guests in an area smaller than 40 square meters? 4 points for yes; add 2 points if it was more than sixteen guests; 0 for no; -2 if you never entertain guests or have always lived in a larger area.

16. Do you know what Wódka Żołądkowa Gorzka is? 1 points for yes, add 1 point if you like it, 0 for no.

17. Have you ever ridden in a *mały Fiat*? 4 points for yes; 0 for no; -2 if you don't know what one is.

18. Have you ever pushed a broken-down *mały Fiat* down the street? 5 points for yes; add 2 points if you had to leave it at the side of the road; 0 for no

42 points or more: Congratulations. You're outrageously Polish. Even more Polish than the Poles.

24 to 41 points: You're very Polish. In fact, check your passport.

11 to 23: You're fairly Polish and have great potential. Whatever you're doing, do it some more.

1 to 10: You're only a smidgen Polish but there's always hope. Try harder.

0 to -12: You're negative Polish which means you're fresh off the boat or just very very foreign (good thing you bought this book). But it also might mean you're pathetic. Try to get out more.

Some Behaviors

⑨ Enigmatic Ice Breakers

What does it mean to have a simple conversation? What are the social conventions? What do you say in order to sound like your mental faculties are intact and you're not a social deviant? As an American sociolinguist transplanted to Poland, I often ask myself these questions and find myself fascinated by some pretty mundane stuff. For example, what are the social consequences of responding to the simple question of "How are you?" or in Polish, *Co słychać*? (What's new?)

During my first few years in Poland, my level of Polish was somewhere around Advanced Tarzan. It was enough to get me by in most social interactions but like many language learners, I often made the natural mistake (and still do) of using my foreign language in the same way I would at home.

For example, if a friendly Polish acquaintance asks me, *Co słychać*? (What's new?) my initial reaction is to produce a chipper *Dobrze!* (Fine!) even though I haven't slept, my dog is sick and someone stole my wallet. That's adhering to an American conversational routine: When someone asks, "How are you?" the conventional answer is "Fine." Usually, this is nothing more than just a conversational opener or a simple routine greeting. So it's okay to say, "I'm fine" rather than stopping to explain that your kid broke her arm and the mechanic is charging an outrageous sum to fix your car. An American who says, "I'm fine" in spite of acute misery is simply heeding a cultural convention. However, the person might reveal later on in the conversation that he or she is sick, tired or unhappy. Americans just don't kick off a conversation with down-in-the-dumps news.

In Polish culture, however, greeting and opening a conversation with a friendly soul follows different rules. Rudimentary greetings usually involve a couple of *dzień dobry*'s (hello's) and head-noddings in the hallway. Sometimes I throw in a *pan* (sir) or *pani* (madam) to be extra polite. Sometimes successfully opening a conversation lies in complaining. In response to *"Co słychać?"* (What's new?) Poles (and their European neighbors) expect a meatier exchange to take place and are more likely than Americans to reveal the less glamorous side of life ("The weather is awful and I think I'm getting sick"). That is to say, the God-Awful Truth is more socially acceptable in the initial stages of conversation with Poles than with Americans. Reviewing the imperfections of life can even be a sign of affection.

I walked into a friend's office, feeling like hell with the flu. When she asked me how I was, I croaked my usual *dobrze* (fine). Noticing how terrible I looked, she asked why I had said I was fine and I replied,

"Because I'm American." She expressed her pity (because I was sick, not because I'm an American) and begged me to take care of myself. I appreciated her concern and wouldn't have experienced it without revealing my woes.

Years ago during my first year in Poland, my elderly neighbor (with whom I normally exchanged bare-bones salutations) greeted me warmly in the hallway and added with a shake of her head, "They've turned the water off again." Recognizing the convention, I replied overenthusiastically with my Tarzan grammar that yes, it's terrible! It seems to happen often in our building! We exchanged a few more friendly words and I went on my way, thrilled with one of my first successful and culturally appropriate interactions.

Now I've adapted, and practice more Polish initial exchanges with Polish friends and acquaintances. If I'm stressed, worried or sick, I just say so. If I'm feeling pretty good, I usually just say, "Things are okay." In my adjustment to Polish culture, I've become more truthful earlier in the conversation.

This isn't to say that Poles are forthright purveyors of veracity and Americans are hypocritical, superficial liars. Or that all Poles are depressive cranks and all Americans are excessive optimists. But we all cling to ingrained cultural behaviors—even in the most ordinary situations. We are all just seeking comfortable contact and a familiar way in to conversation, whether it means complaining about hassles at work now—or later.

⊚ The #1 Question

"So what's your story?" an American in Poland demanded a few seconds after we met. I knew exactly what kind of information he wanted. He was simply taking a short cut to questions Americans typically ask when they first meet someone: "Where are you from? What do you do? How long have you lived here? What about your family?" Racking up the answers to these vital questions helps us get to know someone. But when we ask Poles these questions, they feel like they're being interrogated.

Recently, some Poles complained to me about this barrage of queries they get from Americans. I was dumb-founded. Isn't it flattering and gracious when someone asks you all about yourself? Apparently not.

Americans ask questions to show interest and find common ground with someone new—that is, to get to know someone. Then, that person reciprocates by asking questions too. There's also a second pattern: You talk about yourself, and the other person responds in kind. Both techniques serve the common goal of ease in sociability. Granted, there are always egotistical boors for whom "mutual interest" is an alien concept, but let's chalk that up to a lack of sophistication.

Conversational style depends on personality, background, and, of course, culture. American sociolinguist Deborah Tannen dubbed a common feature of New York conversational style "machine-gun questions"—a rat-a-tat-tat series of questions to show interest and involvement in conversation. Of course, not everybody likes or feels comfortable with this style but this is the way some Americans approach new Polish acquaintances.

"Americans ask a lot of questions," warns the culture section of a handbook written by Poles for Poles going to the States to teach and study. "Some of these questions may seem uninformed or elementary. You may be asked very personal questions by someone you have just met." But don't take offense, the handbook advises, "no impertinence is intended." In other words, when Americans confound you with intrusive nosiness, they're just trying to be nice and friendly.

The number one question asked by Americans to new acquaintances—"What do you do?"—might sound a little odd to Poles if it comes out of nowhere. For a long time, work was not considered a source of self-satisfaction in Poland and therefore no guarantee of fruitful conversation. To some extent, this is still true today. And *news flash!* there *are* other topics far more interesting than work.

Unfortunately, this puts me at a loss for something to say when I meet someone. What should I ask then? "What's your shoe size? Do you like dogs? What did you have for lunch today?" This just doesn't cut it on a social level.

The key is not to rely heavily on questions to jump-start a conversation. Some Poles find a rapid-fire series of questions annoying, although some do find it flattering, and say Americans are open and friendly. But they have other ways of getting to know someone. I used to ask Poles a lot of personal questions and then wonder why they didn't reciprocate. Sometimes, I felt a little hurt and then started to worry that my personality is so lackluster that it piques little interest. If they do want to ask something personal, they sometimes say, "Sorry, can I ask you a personal question?" I say yes of course, bracing myself for an inquiry about my salary, pants size or sex life and they just want to know how I learned my faulty Polish or how long I've been in Poland.

But now I get it. Poles don't usually ask personal questions upon meeting someone. Such queries come later; or personal information is revealed gradually over the course of the conversation. Unlike Americans, Poles don't try to "get to know" someone within the first contact. Over a period of time, they observe you, exchange opinions with you, listen to your stories, problems, jokes and so forth before exchanging personal data.

Seasoned American expatriates are used to this other way of getting to know someone. If someone asks them the short-cut question, "So what's your story?" the answer just might be a shrug, "Ah, I'll tell you later."

⑨ Seeking Therapeutic Friendship

Friendship should be simple and beautiful but that's not always the case when you're looking at friends with a cross-cultural perspective. It can get a little murky.

First, there's the Polish-English word issue: In English, we have the blanket term "friend" for just about anyone we know. In Polish, there's *znajomy* (an acquaintance, a term used often that doesn't sound stilted), *kolega* (like a colleague but in a warmer sense) and sometimes, you might hear *kumpel* (a pal or buddy). The word *przyjaciel* (friend) is used less often and reserved for very close friends. Americans seem to do all right by Polish standards in the casual rankings but when it comes to the *Przyjaciel* Category, the perception is that they're a bit deficient.

In *American Cultural Patterns*, authors Edward C. Stewart and Milton J. Bennett say that Americans "rarely form deep and lasting friendships in which friends become mutually dependent upon each other." Compared to other cultures, there's an "American reluctance to become deeply involved with other persons." The authors add that while members of other cultures might turn to friends for help and comfort, Americans trot down to the shrink's office rather than burdening friends with troubles. An overstatement, in my opinion, but there's no denying that the therapy business flourishes in the U.S. So what if we want to talk to a stranger about our dysfunctional-manic-depressive-inner-child feelings of low self-esteem and alienation? You *would* have to pay somebody to listen to that.

It seems that some Poles are mystified or disappointed by friendships with Americans. I caught hell for not keeping in regular enough contact with a Polish couple whom I'm very fond of. The next time I saw the husband, he told me, "My wife is pissed off with you," and explained that he's spent years trying to convince her that Americans *can* form solid friendships. I called and groveled.

When Poles consider you a *przyjaciel* or *kolega* but you haven't been in touch, they might let you know they miss you by making affectionate ironic statements. Something like, "I'm just calling to make sure you're still alive." Recently, some Polish friends told my husband that they couldn't remember what I looked like anymore. But the thing is, I had thought that we were in pretty good contact considering how busy we all are.

A Polish friend who seemed to drop off the face of the earth called recently. "I'm being American. I have no time," she sighed. Another Pole complained that he was working so much that he was too busy to see his friends, "Like an American," he said.

What might be misleading is that many Americans are perceived as friendly, outgoing and open but this doesn't mean that they are committed. Maybe that's what's disappointing to Poles. Americans form deep and lasting friendships just like anyone else over a long period of time—just longer than what Poles expect. I suspect that a Polish relationship just reaches a level of intimacy faster. Or, perhaps, as one American surmises, "Americans are more used to casual low-maintenance friendships." All this fits the value Americans place on self-reliance and independence; depending on somebody regularly is to be avoided but, nonetheless, it does happen between very intimate friends.

I also have the impression the Poles keep contact with their friends and buddies more often. Of course, everybody in the world has a million things to do, but it seems that even very busy Poles keep in closer contact with friends than busy Americans do. I wonder if therapists are hard-pressed for business here.

⑨ Breezy Easy

A Polish woman was attending a formal meeting at a ministry. On the table was a plate of cookies. She asked about taking one but someone told her, "No, don't bother. They've been there for ten years."

That is one lonely plate of cookies. So many Poles passed through that room and not one ventured to snag a goodie? Wow. An American would probably just take one. Heck, why not? Why else is there food sitting out?

This American approach contributes to our reputation as a breezy and casual tribe of people. If we want to do something simple like eat a cookie, we just do it, right?

Americans come off as informal because we don't hesitate or wait to do what we perceive as mundane things. We'll stroll into people's offices, living rooms, and kitchens, and when really comfortable, we might even open someone's fridge. We'll shrug off our coats, sit down,

maybe prop a foot up on the rung of chair. And, unlike in the aforementioned cookie situation, we'll dig into food placed in the realm of public consumption.

All that sounds unremarkable except that it's the opposite of how many Poles behave. They'll often hesitate or simply wait to be invited before doing such "small" things. And because of this, Americans might perceive them as formal, stiff or shy.

A Polish woman who is used to hosting Poles as well as foreigners describes Polish habits this way: "You have to tell Poles what to do. They wait for invitations and expect to be encouraged." For example, she had some people over for a spontaneous lunch: "They came in, I had to say, 'Put your coats here, go to the big room over there and sit down.' I served them sandwiches and went back to the kitchen. Then I had to tell them to start eating since they were waiting for me to join them." Foreigners, she says, "don't hesitate. They're invited over so they just come in. The sandwiches are for them, so they just eat."

Another behavior that fuels the American easy breezy reputation is how they strike up conversations with strangers. After attending a large, American cocktail party, a Polish businessman admired how fluidly Americans socialize with new people. "I know American culture but I still don't know how to do that. It makes me envious," he says. The big difference here is Americans will say hello and introduce themselves while Poles usually wait to be introduced. Americans also move around the room to mingle and get to know a variety of people—a concept I've found myself explaining to some Poles.

Americans' body language (like leaning or draping extremities on furniture), smiling, and using first names right off the bat rounds out the picture of ease. Again all of that contrasts with typical Polish behavior: People sit up straight, they smile less, and in some cases, still use titles.

At first, Americans might find Poles stilted or overly-formal. In *American Cultural Patterns,* authors Edward C. Stewart and Milton J. Bennett say that folks who behave formally "are judged by Americans to be stuffy." The authors say that in American culture, "No higher compliment can be paid to an important person than the statement, 'He's a regular guy—real down to earth.' That is, we want to treat everyone—and be treated—the same. People tip-toeing around each other is not a component of regular guy- and galness and Poles often do it when an "important person," like a boss, is in the room. However, such hierarchical behavior is starting to disappear among younger Poles.

Of course, Americans might come off a little too casual or overconfident and that can be interpreted as a lack of respect or manners. Other cultures might have difficulty understanding that for Americans, "acting naturally" and not expecting (or giving) special treatment is an expression of mutual respect—allowing others the space and freedom to act how they want.

But here's the good news: Many Poles say they admire the "confidence" and ease of Americans; it's an expression of freedom and directness. "Poles accept it as a cultural difference," says the Pole who reported the cookie incident.

And, many Americans grow to appreciate the way that discreet Polish formalities reflect respect. An American woman says, "We admire it because it's so considerate of other people's presence and reactions, that you're not barging in."

Hey! At some level here, I think we have some cross-cultural understanding. Let's all go out for milk and cookies.

⑨ The Big But

Two Polish friends were having a disagreement over the definition of a word in Polish. Their spat was making me uneasy. They consulted a dictionary but then quarreled over the word's implications. When I tried to change the subject, they ignored me. Finally, the conversation eased into another topic as if nothing had happened. The only person rattled by the little battle was me—the American.

The clash bothered me because I am used to a non-confrontational style of talk. When Americans spot an argument down the road, they usually grab the conversational steering wheel and veer off to a safer topic. Poles, however, often don't mind a head-on collision of opinions. Instead, disagreements are treated as a natural part of talk.

An American expert in language-teaching points out that Americans seek harmony in conversation. There are even certain recognized taboo topics—politics, religion and sex—that you don't bring up unless you feel confident that others think similarly. It is pleasant, polite and proper to agree, especially with those you don't know so well.

Heads nodding in unison over shared opinions and common ground reap good-willed rapport.

Americans put on kid gloves when it comes to disagreeing (intimate relationships excepted of course). A text-book for learners of American English says: "Notice that you need to be very polite when disagreeing with someone in English—even someone you know quite well." Appropriate phrases are: "I see what you mean, but...," I guess you could say that, but...," and "Well, you have a point there, but..." In other words, it's important to validate the other person's opinion before getting down and dirty with the Big But.

A Polish acquaintance and I were talking about Prague. I explained that while I enjoyed the architecture, I didn't like the atmosphere because of too many tourists. It was better to live in Warsaw. "Well, you're wrong, but that's your opinion," she said. I felt as if I had been slapped. By Polish standards, I was overreacting.

Poles spar easily with each other and don't tiptoe around tiffs. Differences don't threaten rapport; they kindle colorful conversation. Plus, as one Pole notes, "Disagreements aren't taken so personally." Besides, it's also one way of really getting to know someone. You can talk about politics, religion and sex (usually in that order, says a Pole) and don't have to do any fancy tap-dancing around a disagreement. Edmund Ronowicz, a Polish linguist at Macquarie University, Australia, says that "Poles will not hesitate to use a straightforward *Nie!* (No!) to disagree during an informal argument." Similarly, you might hear *Wcale nie!* (No way!), *To jest bez sensu!* (That's nonsense!), or *Ja się nie zgadzam!*" (I disagree!). But there is a limit. When civility is lost and a loud circular argument drags on with everyone talking at the same time, social acceptability plummets.

There seems to be a continuum of disagreement styles; one end is non-challenging and the other is confrontational. In *Black and White Styles in Conflict*, Thomas Kochman compares white and black behavior in public debates: "The black mode...is high-keyed: animated, interpersonal and confrontational. The white mode—that of the middle class—is relatively low-keyed: dispassionate, impersonal, and non-challenging."

In *You Just Don't Understand,* a book on gender differences in conversation, sociolinguist Deborah Tannen says that among girls, "agreeing and being the same are ways to create rapport. Excelling, being different, and fighting are threats to rapport. The boys are buying rapport too but they buy it with a different currency: They don't fear disagreement, and they don't seem to need to declare themselves the same."

It seems that the Poles' style of disagreement leans toward that dynamic style. Americans usually try to avoid disagreement or engage in a non-challenging padded exchange. This means Americans might mistake the Poles for contentious souls at times. But the other side is worrisome too: Maybe some Poles find Americans just downright boring.

⑨ Scoring Help

All I wanted to do was thank my Polish hosts for their hospitality, hop in a taxi and go home. That seemed pretty simple—I had done it before without incident. However, my friends wanted to leave their cozy apartment on a freezing cold night to drive me home. I insisted on calling a cab and an argument ensued. I was apparently coming off as an obnoxiously independent American.

This was not the first time I have been scolded by Poles for not requesting or refusing help. But the fact is Americans often hesitate before asking or accepting favors from other people. These are uncomfortable and face-threatening acts; a dependence on others is an admission that "I can't do it myself." Agony! Self-reliance and autonomy are esteemed personality traits; asking for help cramps the American style. Poles, on the other hand, will easily ask friends and family for help. Depending on others can be an affirmation of friendship and sometimes, it's simply necessary.

When I was sick with the flu, I holed up in my apartment for days, dug through the dregs of the fridge for food and slept like a bear. Later, a Polish relative who lives nearby was obviously irritated that she didn't know I was ill—why didn't I call her? She would have been happy to bring me soup, make me tea and fluff my pillows. Okay, that would have been nice, but it never occurred to me to pick up the phone. It would have been admitting that I can't take care of myself and I certainly wouldn't have wanted to impose on her.

And there's the key: the notion of imposition. God forbid that we should be a bother to anyone—above all, our friends. It's as if there's some big Scoreboard of Imposition and the winning personality is the one with the fewest points racked up. Asking for a favor American-style often includes some sort of expression to show we don't wish to impose: "I hope it's not too much to ask...," "If you don't mind...," or "If it's not a problem..." These types of formulas are even used between close friends. We give people an easy out so the person doesn't feel pressured: "...if you can't, that's okay," or "if not, I understand."

This is not the case with Poles. Need is regarded as normal, so favors are easily exchanged. And it's natural (and sometimes necessary) to depend on friends for rides, errands, babysitting, shopping, lodging and telephone use. A friend without a car couldn't get a babysitter at the last minute so her friend drove across town to pick up the kid for an overnight stay. The next day, she ferried the kid back home. Wow. Would an American ask someone to do that? I doubt it, unless it was planned out a week in advance.

The Polish way to ask a favor doesn't usually convey the idea of imposition between friends. Rather, a Pole might stress the importance or urgency of the request ("It's really important") or what a great pal you can be ("It'd be really nice if you could..."). The assumption is that the friend will understand and agree willingly. Sometimes, Poles have appeared almost aggressive when they've told me "You're the only one I can ask," which might very well be true, but more likely is meant to show me what an important and helpful friend I am.

The notion of impingement is communicated between Poles when people don't know each other well or when there's a difference in status. When I taught at the University of Warsaw, my students often prefaced their requests for help with "I'm sorry to take up your time," or "I hope I'm not imposing but..." I used to find it strange since it was my job but this is the Polish social convention when making a request of someone of superior status.

Then there's the issue of what an offer of help means. Once a Polish friend stopped in for a surprise visit and found me in a tizzy. I was very busy, had tons of work piled up and still needed to clean my messy apartment before guests arrived for the weekend. "It looks as if you need some help," she said, peering into one disaster area. She offered to do my dishes and mop the floor. I felt a little embarrassed and even indignant that she thought I couldn't do it on my own. Also, the thought of someone finding out how much scum could accumulate on my kitchen floor horrified me. I refused her offer. Of course, she wasn't questioning my ability to cope but expressing her affection for me in the form of a soapy dishrag.

Since life isn't chock-full of consumer conveniences in Poland, people depend on friends and family to get by. In the States, if you can't manage on your own, you call the babysitter, the taxi driver, the furniture movers, the cleaning service, the delivery person, or the personal shopper. We have quite a developed service industry to take care of these things and we can pay through the nose to maintain our independence. Once these things become widespread and affordable in Poland, it will be interesting to see if the Polish network of favors becomes less prevalent.

About calling a taxi that freezing cold night: My friends finally told me that I was stubborn and stupid. I may be stubborn about my independence, but I'm not stupid: They drove me home.

⑨ Summons on the Rebound

Some friends called to invite my husband and me over for drinks by saying, "Your membership is about to expire so you had better renew." Whoa! What else could we do but accept? From the Polish point of view, they were merely assuring regular contact with beloved friends. From the American point of view, they were applying social pressure. This is because invitations from Poles to their homes are as serious as tax notices; if you don't respond appropriately, be prepared to pay a heavy price.

Americans can appear vague and light-hearted about extending invitations. Poles, among many other nationalities, complain bitterly about the apparent insincerity of the American suggestion "We should get together sometime": the invitation that never materializes. Or—this is where the confusion comes in—it's not an invitation at all! It's just an indication that the person likes you. Many Americans wouldn't consider "Let's get together sometime" a concrete invitation. The word "sometime" is the tip-off; a *real* invitation includes a date, time and place and requires a response.

Sometimes Americans extend an invitation with an "out" ("It's OK if you can't"), a linguistic device to clarify that no social pressure is involved. In the novel *White Noise* by Don DeLillo, a character invites a couple over for dinner and then adds, "I'm not preparing anything major, so just call beforehand and tell me if something else came up. You don't even have to call. If you don't show up, I'll just know that something came up and you couldn't let me know. We have till next May or June to do this thing so there's no special mystique about a week from Saturday." Talk about pressure-free. This is an exaggeration, but something in it rings true for every American.

Invitations from Polish friends to their home, on the other hand, fall into the rock-solid category and they prefer a crystal-clear acceptance in return. If they don't get an unadulterated "yes," they might just feel hurt or maybe ask again to communicate clearly that your charming company is deeply desired. Any hesitation on your part seems to trigger some sort of Polish Rebound action; they keep shooting 'til they score. They'll even help you organize your time so that you can accept. I turned down an invitation for a Sunday morning outing to do some things at home. My friend said, "Why don't you come with us and do your things in the afternoon?" Heavens. What a difference from the laid-back American "Yeah, well, if you can make it, great."

When North Americans don't want to commit time or offend someone with a direct refusal, they resort to the Western Waffle. This means saying something like "Maybe I'll be there," or "I don't know, I'll let you know." We hate saying "no" directly; it just sounds so, um, negative. Notice how well this complements the it's-OK-if-you-can't mentality. Also notice the head-on collision with the Polish Rebound style.

A Canadian was invited by Polish friends to a wedding two months away. Unsure, he indicated that *maybe* he would attend, which of course just activated the Polish Rebound effect. They checked again and again to see if he would be there, which then caused him to employ the Western Waffle over and over. In the end, he wasn't at the wedding and apparently his friends felt hurt. A North American would have picked up on the signals of non-commitment and wouldn't have pressed for an answer.

What makes invitations so fascinating is that both Poles and Americans gripe about their own invite systems. I asked a Pole to explain how to turn down an invitation graciously. "You don't, there's no way," she sighed, "This is the problem." Apparently, the excuse has to be specific and air-tight. Another Pole says she resents having to turn linguistic somersaults just to assure the person that it's sincere. But the funny thing is if you send out a written R.S.V.P. or Regrets Only invitation for more formal affairs in Poland, you can't count on a response. Oral invitations carry more weight.

As for Americans, the let's-do-lunch-sometime syndrome has become a joke. And the meaning of "We should get together sometime" doesn't rank much higher. One American complained, "That phrase should go in the dictionary and the meaning should be 'I don't ever want to see you again.'"

Maybe that's why some Americans use printed invitations ("You're Invited!") more than Poles. Like tax notices, Americans want it in writing.

⟲ Proper Chowing Down

The mention of "table manners" makes most of us nervous. Should I scrub soup stains off my shirt at the table? Or just act as If I enjoy big spots? If I inhale a piece of meat and can't speak, should I gesture desperately toward my throat? Or just smile and choke gracefully? Of course, the answers to these question depend on which manners you follow: Continental or American.

Rules for prescribed "proper" behavior are attention nabbers, as if it's a litmus test ("Am I a cretin?"). As most people know, "good manners" is nothing more than consideration for others. But some rules of etiquette are simply arbitrary codes to convey that you weren't born in a barn. For example, in the States, there's a little known rule about an unoccupied hand at the table: it should not rest on the table but on your lap. But careful! In Poland, both hands from the wrists up should be kept above the table at all times. Another difference: Americans eat with the fork in the right hand but will pass it to the left hand in order to cut with a knife in the right. Then they return the fork to the right to eat. Phew! Lots of work. Continental style means fork in the left hand, tines usually face down, and pushing food onto the fork with the knife in the right.

There's nothing inherently "polite" about how you manage unoccupied hands, forks and tines. Of course Yankee utensil maneuvers might draw a little attention. But I doubt that any Pole is going to judge you as a thoughtless uncultured lug if you hold your fork in, eek!, the right hand or even place your hands in your lap at the table. As long as you're not flipping peas into people's faces or doing anything naughty with your hands below the table, you'll probably get invited back.

However, if you don't follow some other basic Polish table manners, you might invite judgement regarding your "consideration for others." Here's one danger area: autonomy. Americans don't mind serving themselves. If you want something, you ask for it or take it. Casual and independent. Kinda sums up the whole country right there at the table. Poles, by contrast, will *always* serve others (women and guests first) or wait to be served. That means that, even under casual circumstances, Americans could wind up looking *niekulturalny* (Cretin City) if they innocently refill their own glass.

Of course, most people know it's oafish to grab the last serving. Americans just do less of a song and dance about it. The Polish way requires more of a show. Poles might joke, *Czy mamy zgasić światło?* (Should we turn the lights off?) to protect the identity of the one who eats the last cutlet. If you want the last of something, act like you don't. Insist that someone else take it, and if you're lucky, no one will accept. Or if it's offered to you, refuse and then finally act like you're taking it only because the person insists—or more selflessly, because you hate waste.

Utensil codes can help you at peoples' homes or a restaurant. Lay your knife and fork parallel on the side of your plate to show that you have finished licking it clean (it's polite to polish off every crumb to show you liked it). But if you want to continue eating, make an X by crossing the knife and fork on your plate which gracefully says, "I'm not done yet, okay?"

When you're finished at the table, it's polite to say, *dziękuję* as you stand up to leave. And, by the way, Poles are highly conscientious about not starting until everyone is served. Though I'm told it's a bit old-fashioned, for a clear green light, you might hear *smacznego* for bon apetit. There's no English equivalent except, perhaps, "Dig in folks!." Of course, well-mannered people know better than to say that. They would say, "Please, dig in."

◎ Stuffing Yourself Silly

Polish hospitality elevates the guest to the status of God for an evening—*Gość w dom, Bóg w dom* (Guest in the home, God in the home) the saying goes. American hospitality, on the other hand, seems to exist on a continuum from full-service to self-service. That is, you might be waited on hand and foot, every need anticipated, or, someone might say, "Beer's in the fridge, help yourself."

There are two ways of hosting in Poland. The traditional way and the "informal" way, practiced by younger Poles and more familiar to Americans. Poles under 40 tend to practice the informal way; older Poles stick more closely to the traditional way.

The traditional way is more structured and as far as I can figure, the rules are: Offer the guests everything in the house again and again; do everything for their comfort; be prepared to shave the family dog if it makes them happy; don't let them leave under any circumstances. The gracious guests' rules are: Sit, eat and drink everything enthusiastically; rave about it; stay for a long time.

American hospitality varies widely from household to household. In some homes, you might stay seated while the host whisks away your empty plate and serves you coffee with milk and sugar—stirred. In other homes, the spirit is expressed by the formulaic phrases "Help yourself" and "Make yourself at home." This suggests that a certain amount of autonomy is acceptable among guests. In these situations, it's polite not to create a fuss or let people fuss over you. You could be invited to help yourself, which might involve getting your own beer and ripping open a bag of potato chips. The younger generation of Poles may not go that far but they do practice the help-yourself approach that their parents might find disrespectful toward guests.

In any case, opening the fridge or dumping your own dirty dish in the sink in a Polish home could be an affront to hosting talents. Hospitality in the U.S. isn't quite the art form it is in Poland. For this reason, it's strikingly pleasant for Americans to enter a Polish home.

As a guest in the Polish household, it's difficult to go wrong with politeness. If you are offered something to eat or drink, it's polite to say *tak, proszę* (yes, please) since the successful guest is the guest who consumes. Old World politeness says you can turn the offer down with *dziękuję* and a shake of the head to mean "no thanks," since that provides the person with the opportunity to host to the hilt, reoffering until you say "yes." Stuffing yourself silly is proper behavior. And all hosts assume you are there to behave properly. When you've reached your limit, it takes a series of firm *dziękuję's* (two minimum) to stop the process. The older and more traditional the host, the more assertive the hospitality.

On the flip side, this "yes-no" stuff can get confusing if you are hosting Polish guests. When they say "no thanks" it might be the polite, indirect "yes, please" and you are expected to offer it again. Super-polite Poles are dismayed when they say "no thanks" and the American host whisks food off the table. When Americans say "no thanks" at the dinner table, it usually means "No, I'm full, leave me alone."

Anyway, since a guest in the Polish home is God, He can stay as long as He wants. Who would dare give God the hint to hit the road? Of course, God would be sensitive to the droopy red eyes of the hosts, but it's still up to Him to call it a night with *No, zasiedzieliśmy się*

(Well, we're staying too long). One night my husband and I hosted a Polish couple who stayed and stayed. There was nothing we could do or say. If they had been Americans, I would have had no problem saying, "Well, it's three in the morning, I guess we should call it a night." This would be unforgivably rude by Polish standards. Guests might notice that the evening is starting to come to a close when the barrage of consumables slows down. But this doesn't mean you can just get up and go.

And this is the touchy part.

Guests are not supposed to leave, so any inclination toward the door elicits protests, *Już? Dlaczego? Co wam się tak spieszy?* (Already? Why? What's your hurry?). You stay a little longer and feel guilty when they express their disappointment again, *Nie, jeszcze jest wcześnie* (No, it's still early!). But be reasonable in your reaction—a Polish friend tells me what people really mean is, "If you want to go, our feelings won't be hurt."

When you actually make it to the door, you gush gratitude: *Dziękuję za przyjemny wieczór* (Thank you for the pleasant evening), compliments on the company and food, and maybe a suggestion to meet again at your place. Count on spending more time for this threshold conversation.

Once you finally manage to leave, you're no longer someone special, no longer a guest, no longer God. Heading back home, you revert to your hell-bound self.

⑨ A Host of Talk

There is only one problem with spending marvelous evenings at Polish friends' homes for parties, dinners or drinks: I should be reciprocating these invitations more often. Gulp. Confession: Hosting Poles intimidates me. Can my hosting style ever match up to theirs?

If you have the pleasure to visit a very traditional Polish household, your hosts will pile your plate over with pork chops ("We slaughtered our pig just for your visit!"), handmade pierogi ("Grannie's arthritis doesn't stop her when it comes to guests!"), and homemade jams ("Threw my back out picking these strawberries!"). Even for a casual last-minute get-together, the right types of consumables always seem appear. And, a quick stop-over visit will prompt an offer of coffee or tea within minutes of your crossing the threshold.

Of course, Americans are fine hosts and will serve guests a homemade dinner. But, in the American Culture of Convenience, it's also common to invite people out for dinner in the name of hospitality. Or even, for a more casual affair, buy some take-out food to eat at home. When it comes to friends, my philosophy of hosting comes from the School of Cooking Fast. It ain't fancy because the most important thing to me is that guests talk to each other.

Everyone loves a good spread but American hosts often look more to lively conversation for a successful party. Sometimes at dinner parties, hosts even dictate seating arrangements to cultivate conversational matches. The talented host or hostess hovers around, introducing people and planting seeds in common ground to sprout good talk: "Eugene, meet Morty. You know, both of you have ant farms."

But apparently, this task is not so easy.

Washington Post columnist Judith Martin, better known as Miss Manners, really slams the American social scene: "Education and professional skills are so specialized that we have no common body of reference and can only exchange trade gossip with immediate colleagues. Social turnover is required because we keep repeating ourselves, rather than continuing to develop our ideas." Ouch. It's no wonder hosts play communication match-makers.

37

Polish hosts don't seem fixated on the Sparkling Conversation Issue. They take that for granted at parties. They can turn their attention to two other two essential ingredients—plenty of food and drink. It's not their social responsibility if a guest arrives with zilch to say that night. Also, friendship networks tend to be closer and more tightly knit than American ones. When there is less "social turnover," the host doesn't have as much social engineering to do.

An American magazine article gives common sense advice on party-giving from famous caterers and hosting "experts" like Martha Stewart (who now might have ideas on jailhouse theme parties). It's interesting—much of the counsel focuses on cultivating guest conversation.

First, hosting mavens recommend that you should "do as much as you can ahead" in order to spend time talking with your guests. Then, "don't overdo" the menu— keep it simple and easy to serve so you don't get trapped in the kitchen. By contrast, I've seen Polish hosts (mostly the hostesses) run a relay between the guests and kitchen to crank out a steady stream of food and alcohol (and somehow still manage to talk to their guests).

The ultimate, according to the article, is to hire caterers so your full attention goes to the guests. That's exactly what I do! Except that on my budget it means ordering pizza.

So I'll just admit it: I fall short when it comes to artful and complete hospitality. I'm more comfortable focusing on the talk. I'm afraid if I try to duplicate Polish hosting on a regular basis, I'll have to be hospitalized after every party.

⑨ Public Love

You're shopping in a store and your toddler is getting antsy. A stranger stops for a cootchie-cootchie-coo and pays him a compliment. In the States, maybe you smile, but mainly you check out the person for weirdness, especially if you're in a city. In Poland, you can relax; you're experiencing public love for children.

Americans might be surprised at how kid-friendly Polish society is. Certainly the States provides more child-oriented environments, events and products: amusement parks, kid museums, TV, movies, the raging toy industry (Mickey Mouse is considered a cultural icon). Stores, offices and restaurants have play areas with toys and books to keep Junior occupied while Daddy and Mommy spend their money without distraction. And good old capitalism does drive kid culture—children are a well-targeted consumer group in the U.S. Besides Children's Day (June 1), Poland is not as commercially developed in this area yet, but is more child-oriented in terms of everyday social contact: Children are everyone's concern as a matter of course. Hillary Rodham Clinton would be proud of the Poles' it-takes-a-village attitude in everyday public interactions with children.

The unspoken rule among Americans is that you never tell or even hint to other parents how to raise their children. So when it comes to public life with kids, the social distance is even greater. In the U.S., kiddies in public are purely the charge of the parents. Everybody just backs off.

In Poland, parents treat children like public property, even in the cosmopolitan city of Warsaw. The most glaring example is how strangers (mainly grandma types) on the street will comment on child-care, most often concerning the child's dress. Even in mild fall weather, strangers have told me that my daughter needs a hat, gloves, a scarf, a warmer coat, and in the summer, a sunhat, long sun-blocking sleeves, and sun cream for her face. Once, in the park on a chilly day, an older Polish woman peered into my baby carriage to announce that my baby should be wearing a second hat because of the wind. What wind? There was barely a breeze. Poles see the wind and the cold as deadly enemies, and Polish grandmas have public license to protect children from such evils. They're also fulfilling their own need to act as valuable members of society. Polish mothers resent the controlling element of their advice, but usually shrug it off. One Polish mother says, "I don't like it. I say it's not so cold, don't worry, she's fine." Another says, "I just ignore it."

Comments to strangers about their kids are unthinkable in the U.S., and as an American mother in Poland, I found such comments offensive and paranoia-inducing. There have been times when I put a hat on my daughter just to show the other people in the park that I wasn't trying to kill my child. Now I recognize these comments as a show of concern. Irritating? Yes. But I accept the social dynamic behind it.

Strangers in Poland also go out of their way to make life easier for kids and parents. One of the loveliest experiences for American parents in Poland is the priority assigned to parents with children. Strangers usher child-encumbered parents to the front of the line, especially if the child is a newborn. In a crowded bus, tram or metro, the crowd parts like the Red Sea to free up a seat. Even youths practice this social nicety. After enjoying this Royal Mother with Child treatment in Poland, I arrived at Chicago O'Hare Airport and hauled my exhausted child toward the front of the passport control line for American citizens. I looked expectantly at the faces to see who would offer me a place at the front; impassive looks informed me that I was behaving like a foreigner among my compatriots.

Recently in the waiting room at an animal hospital in Warsaw, I was trying to simultaneously drag my dog to the vet's examination room and convince my stubborn three-year-old to come with me. Watching my struggle, a mother patted an empty seat between her and her daughter and offered to watch my daughter while I hauled my dog in for repairs. I said thanks anyway and explained that my daughter wouldn't stay with a stranger. Such a kind offer from a stranger would be inconceivable in the States.

An American father compares his experience of flying on an American airline with flying on Poland's LOT. His kids were sick on the American plane. "We obviously had chaos going on," he said, "but the flight attendants didn't offer us help." The flight on LOT, meanwhile, was "incomparably different." The kids weren't sick, but the Polish flight attendants were more, well, attendant (for instance, doling out an extra pillow for a kid who couldn't sleep). "It was much more human," the American says.

And strangers on the bus, in the post office, or in a restaurant pay attention to kids simply for the human pleasure of interacting with a child—a comment, a question, or a goofy face. Waiters offer kids colorful drink stirrers, clerks give small gifts. Whether the kid responds, hides out of shyness or cries, it doesn't matter; Poles consider it a natural part of socializing kids.

By contrast, in the States it's rare to address a parent about their child, or to address the child with anything beyond a smile, a look of sympathy or, at the most, a comment in passing such as, "I've been there." The amount of engagement is limited: No one wants to come off as a social intruder or, worse, a kidnapper or molester. Parents indoctrinate kids with "don't talk to strangers" from an early age. They practice and expect distance when it comes to children in public places. I was playing with my daughter in the kiddie museum in my small hometown in Michigan. I helped her climb into a dinosaur costume, and a nearby kid looked interested. I offered to help him with a second costume, and his father was quick to step up and say, "Oh, I'll do that." His reaction and tone told me he was in charge. Maybe he was trying to be a good father, but the message was clear: He didn't want me near his kid.

Besides, there are a lot of non-parents out there, and they are deeply unconcerned about your child; some prefer not to see the scamps in public. In a cafe in the U.S., my daughter burst out into song and clanged her spoon on her plate. I shushed her, but the folks at the next table shot me some tight-lipped looks as if to say, "Keep your brat under control." Poles usually smile to say, "Ain't that cute? Ain't that natural?"

And that's the village point. I find that all kinds of Poles of different ages—parents and non-parents alike—show natural tolerance and affection and engage freely when it comes to little rascals in public settings. The U.S. offers many more child-designated places than Poland does. Families flock to family restaurants, parks and events. It's certainly an advantage—life is easier for parents, and the kids have fun. No country in the world can compete with U.S. entertainment for kids. But entertainment is not socialization. Poles accept and integrate kids into public life whether the kids are cute, grumpy, or shy. It's not showy, you can't sell it, and it's healthy: an understated social advantage of Poland.

Hey Mickey Mouse, take note.

🌀 An Advice Column

"My wife is afraid to drive in Warsaw," an American told a Pole. Leaping into action, the Pole outlined a plan on how to help her get over her fear: Every day she should drive in Warsaw, starting at 4:00 a.m. the first day and then fifteen minutes later each day thereafter. After a few weeks of that, she would learn to manage the traffic little by little. In the American's opinion, that was pretty useless advice. "We would lose too much sleep," he told the Pole.

"Poles love to give advice," several Poles tell me. While there are certainly many insufferable jerks who thrive on establishing a one-up position, many Poles use advice-giving simply to express interest or involvement. A while back, a friendly taxi-driver advised me to buy a car so that I wouldn't go bankrupt paying the escalating fares.

Sometimes Poles just want to share knowledge—even with strangers. While out walking my dog one evening, I made the acquaintance of a neighbor, also out with his dog. We chatted and he wound up advising me to sell my apartment and buy a house with a yard while real estate prices were low outside Warsaw. "That's not really something we want to do," I replied, but he still urged me to think it over.

American sociolinguist Deborah Tannen points out one general difference in male-female communication: When women talk about problems, it's not so much to get advice but more to feel understood and get confirmation for their feelings. Men are socialized to act as problem-solvers, so when they perceive a problem, there is often a knee-jerk reaction of advice-offering and that can annoy some women.

Poles follow the pattern of Tannen's advice-giving men and this behavior is linked to recent history. Poles have been socialized to offer advice and information; for a long time daily life resembled a jigsaw puzzle in which fitting the pieces together was not always a transparent process.

During Communist times, people needed information on how to get through the maze of bureaucracy, and where and how to buy necessities. Collecting advice from several people would often clarify the solution. One Pole told me, "You needed advice 100 times a day. Without advice, you were lost." Today, many Poles feel comfortable passing on helpful information—whether it's solicited or not—without necessarily expecting that it will be accepted.

Americans, on the other hand, are a little touchy about giving and taking advice. To some, unsolicited advice sounds like "Obviously, you don't know what to do and I know better"—a big no-no in a culture in which autonomy and a mind-your-own-business approach are highly valued. Advice is taken well when it is solicited or an advisor's greater experience is recognized. While seeking advice from someone can even be a form of flattery, unsolicited advice is often considered impolite, particularly when the suggestion is unpleasant, difficult or personal such as "You should budget your money more carefully," or "Why don't you lose weight?" When Americans do offer advice, it's often couched in tentative terms such as "Have you thought about..." or "Maybe you could..."

Contrast that with mothers who are used to hearing helpful childcare tips in the streets and parks ("You should be holding the hand of such a small child"). In the States, the mother would have the right to feel insulted or angry.

Some Polish friends warned an American about walking home because of muggings. Maybe they wanted to express concern for the foreigner, but it was his own neighborhood after all (and his choice). "As if I couldn't figure it out myself," he laughed. Maybe he should buy a car they told him. Good idea, but then he would have to get up at 4:00 a.m. to learn how to drive it in Warsaw.

ⓘ Public Heat

While parking my car, I pulled my car farther into the spot to make sure the bike rack on the back didn't stick out into the street. A Polish man stopped to watch and scolded me for parking on the grass—one of the wheels was on a plot of dirt. "That's not grass," I said and he shouted at me. Two other Poles standing on the sidewalk confirmed that it was indeed just dirt. An argument broke out and I walked away.

Poles don't enjoy public confrontations but they don't shy away from them either. If they feel that someone has threatened their personal pride or property, or done something wrong or stupid, they'll argue with or even yell at a stranger in public.

By contrast, most Americans tend to avoid public clashes—or approach them less directly.

Take driving. Everybody knows how driving enhances people's personalities. Americans usually lay on the horn and swear and gesture inside the safety of their car. In Warsaw, a guy could leap out of his car and stomp up to your car. After I passed through an intersection with no traffic signs, a taxi driver followed me to where I parked a short distance away. He got out of his car and informed me *most* un-

47

pleasantly that I had turned when he had the right-of-way (and he was correct). In the worst case, a guy might even yank open your car door so that you can better hear him rant about your driving. The insults get pretty creative ("If you're afraid to drive this expensive car, why don't you buy yourself a wheelbarrow?!").

When chewing over the reasons for these occasional public frays, many Poles say their temperament is emotional and explosive, "like the Italians'." A confrontation can billow to dramatic dimensions and just as quickly blow over. Explaining why she initiated an angry clash in a restaurant, a young Polish woman shrugged it off, "I just couldn't help myself."

Americans are startled and threatened by such outbursts; for a Pole, it just means you're angry. That's not unreasonable; it's just unpleasant and perhaps necessary.

I once witnessed an argument between a Polish colleague and an older man outside a public office. When my colleague said he was next in line, the man started to boil, "That's not true! You aren't in the right order!" "I was keeping track of my place!" my co-worker argued. A woman joined in, "If you hadn't been so busy talking, you'd have seen you weren't in line at all!" My colleague stuck to his guns and entered the office. Then on his way out, he shouted at the man, "Next time, keep track of who's in front of you in line!"

Why the emotional bombs? Some Poles blame leftovers from the old system—the pent-up anger and hair-tearing frustrations of everyday life. How you were treated personally in mundane situations took on a greater significance. And usually it is middle-aged or older Poles who initiate the shouting matches. If you don't state your position with emotion and force, it signals that you're without resolve—and therefore not credible. Other Poles say it's more important to stand up for your rights than to be polite. Going on the offensive shows that you can stand up for yourself and don't take crap from people.

Americans would rather back down or walk away than get embroiled in a public shouting match. The cultural needs for surface courtesy and emotional control usually prevail. Someone who makes a scene in public comes off as irrational (or maybe as a New Yorker-type who relishes a little give-and-take). Sure, people might exchange angry words with a stranger but it's less intense; losing your cool and shouting at someone means there's something wrong *with you*.

So if Americans are less intense in public confrontations, it could also mean that some go home with regrets like, "Damn! I shoulda said, 'Are you having a bad day or is this your personality?' Yeah, I shoulda said that..."

Many Poles, mainly older ones, overestimate the amount of emotional energy necessary to get their message across and are surely blowing off steam about other frustrations. Younger Poles can stand up for themselves in public too but don't blow up so easily, especially over small things. These days they have other ways to spend their energy.

⑨ Verbal Strokes

A Polish friend told me that my Polish had improved, so I said thank you. "Oh, that wasn't a compliment," he corrected me, "It's just an observation."

Compliments are what one sociolinguist calls "social lubricant." They promote good will and establish solidarity between people—an indication that you like the same things, have some common ground, and belong to the same group in some way.

Naturally, people enjoy kind words and ways of complimenting vary. Supposedly, women offer praise more frequently than men and—no surprise—women also give and receive compliments on appearance more often. When acknowledging compliments, some people just say thank you (demurely or delightedly) but there's a risk that if you agree wholeheartedly, it sounds likes bragging. Very often out of embarrassment or modesty, people deny or undermine compliments. The cliché is the woman who receives a compliment on a dress and responds, "Oh, this ol' rag?" Then there are the types who deny compliments at length, which serves to focus the conversation on the compliment.

And, reactions to admiring words differ from culture to culture. Telling an Apache Indian or a Thai that you like something of theirs might be interpreted as a request for the person to give it to you. This could cut down on shopping time, but what happens when you say, "Oh, what a beautiful baby!"?

Members of other cultures are sometimes surprised at how often Americans give compliments. After examining over 1000 examples of compliments by Americans, one linguist concluded that Americans use compliments for other things besides establishing solidarity. A compliment may be used to express gratitude ("That was a great dinner") or to soften criticism ("You did a great job except...") which might be perceived as hypocritical. Sometimes, we even use laudatory statements to open conversations ("I enjoyed your talk," or "Nice car"). American educators depend heavily on praise to encourage students' work. Some people think this is a great way to build students' self-esteem; other think it produces overconfident types.

Polish sociolinguist Adam Jaworski collected 250 examples of compliments between Poles and concluded that their verbal strokes serve other functions in addition to offering praise. Poles might seek information about the price and place of purchase of something ("That's nice, where did you get it?") or tease each other through compliments (like a back-handed compliment: "You look good with that spaghetti sauce on your face"),

Jaworski also says, "Compliments in Polish are often treated with suspicion." So a Pole might deny that a given comment was a compliment, to clarify that it's not false flattery or a *pusty komplement* (empty compliment). You also might hear someone say. *To nie komplement. To prawda.* (That's not a compliment. It's the truth) as if compliments are naturally on shaky ground. It's like my friend who complimented—oops, sorry *observed*—my progress in Polish.

Poles sometimes give wry responses as a witty way to deflect a compliment— I told a Polish friend with a new spiffy haircut how great she looked with short hair. "You didn't think I looked good with long hair?" she asked.

⊚ Shhhhhhh!

During a dead-still traffic jam, I sat in a car with a Polish friend who fell silent, obviously irritated with our immobility. I felt compelled to fill up the weighty silence with lively and entertaining chatter. But since I was tired and grumpy too, my noble efforts resulted in empty blather. She finally turned to me and said gently, "If you don't feel like talking, you don't have to." Caught! Red-handed! Making filler small talk. It would have been okay to say nothing. But as an American, I find that even three or four seconds of silence in the presence of another seems like a tortured eternity.

Different cultures regard silence in different ways. Most Western cultures prefer talk over silence, but in Northern European and American Indian cultures, for example, silence can be positive. And of course, silence between couples or good friends can be a sign of intimacy.

Poles, like Americans, value conversation highly, but I have observed some subtle differences between the two groups regarding silence.

At an American dinner party, if the table falls silent when food is served, it's not uncommon to hear someone say, "Oh, now it's quiet, everybody is eating," simultaneously apologizing for and filling in the empty social space. A skilled host or hostess will prevent silence by "keeping up" the conversation. This is regarded as social success—a person who always has something to say.

Brief silences during conversation do not seem to pose as great a threat to Poles. The other night with several Poles, one of these short conversational lulls occurred between topics. To me it was a long spooky pause but when I caught the hostess's eye, she just smiled; it wasn't a social calamity. People may gather their thoughts (and light a cigarette, take a drink) without pressure to fill in the brief conversational gap.

As one Pole put it, "Poles are not as skilled as Americans at making friendly noises," but I disagree. Among Poles, it's acceptable that people not have something to say every second of time spent together—a rather intimate notion. The Polish pace of conversation seems to vary more; a lot of overlapped talk, excited interruptions and sometimes a short lull, as opposed to the more regular stream of talk that Americans feel comfortable sustaining.

I asked an American if he thought Poles were more tolerant of silence than Americans and he responded, "Gosh, I don't know; if there's a lapse in conversation, I always try to fill it up." Bingo. I believe Americans have a lower tolerance for breaks in conversation. Quiet signals the brink of social failure. Pauses longer than even one second can cause uneasiness, so before it becomes unbearable, we quickly stuff some talk into the conversational crack to avert social disaster. Poles seem to tolerate a slightly larger gap in talk before it becomes necessary to shovel in the chatter.

In *The Power of Silence,* sociolinguist Adam Jaworski gives some advice regarding what we experience as awkward pauses: "Communicators should not avoid uncomfortable moments in conversation, but should learn to be comfortable with them and use them to find really important points in conversation." He also advises refraining from what might be "uncomfortable talk."

Jaworski also notes the different expressions for silence in the Polish language. For example, *być cicho* (to be silent) signals the absence of general sound which is different from the verb for the absence of speech, *milczeć* (to be silent or to refrain from speaking), something my traffic-jam partner in the car that day wished to experience in my presence. I think in English we would refer to such a situation using the verb "to shut up."

🌀 Unbridled Hilarity

We all know the situation of listening to somebody tell a joke and then, when the punch-line is delivered—horrors! We don't get it! The brain races, "Do I laugh? If not, I'll offend the person—or maybe even look dumb." This situation is even more apt to happen when somebody from another culture tells us a joke. Since humor is often culture-dependent, the punch line might make no sense, but we all want to be polite and look half-way intelligent. So even if our instinct is to scratch our heads and furrow our brows, we chuckle.

When we don't understand a joke or a funny story, a great face-saving strategy is to say "hah!," smile brightly, and hope for a change in topic. But we risk missing out on the cultural information embedded in the humor. It takes bravery and curiosity to say, "I don't get it." But it's worth it.

A Polish friend told me a joke about the chicken who crossed the road (really). A big truck came rumbling down the street at high speed and ran over the hen, who went rolling to the side of the road. She picked herself up and said *Szatan a nie kogut*! (That was a devil, not a rooster!). *That's funny,* my friend assured me when she saw the blank look on my face. "Duh," I responded. My non-agrarian background has deprived me of an understanding of how hens and roosters have sex. Ask your local chicken farmer for details.

Another Polish friend told me this one: Beyond seven mountains, seven forests, seven rivers, (*Za siedmioma górami, za siedmioma lasami, za siedmioma rzekami...*), a little elf woke up from his sleep, stretched, yawned, took a look around and said, "Damn, how far away I live!" (note: That's the punchline). My friend looked crushed when all I could muster in response was a dopey, hopeful, nervous grin. Here's the key: Polish fairy tales start with this formulaic beyond-seven-mountains stuff, the equivalent of our "Once upon a time..." Nobody expects a mildly vulgar punchline to follow the intro to a fairy tale. A real side-splitter—if you get it.

One formula in Polish which clearly signals the beginning of a joke goes: *Przychodzi baba do lekarza...* (An old woman goes to the doctor...). It's the same for Americans who recognize what level of joke is coming when we hear, "A traveling salesman arrives at a farmhouse..." or "A gorilla walks into a bar..."

Joel Achenbach, who wrote the column "Why Things Are" for *The Washington Post,* answers the question "Why is humor funny?" He says that "the comic effect is usually the result of a conflict between overlapping but incompatible frames of reference" (he's usually not so serious about humor, but that's beside the point). For us foreigners in Poland, many jokes told by Poles are laughable only if we have the proper frames of cultural reference to understand the incompatibility.

In that light, consider this example: These days in Poland, along with inspectors who ask to see tickets on the tram, priests are asking to see crucifixes (note: har-har). People who are aware of the intrusion of the Polish church in everyday life get the joke and snicker. Those without the proper frame of reference don't understand the irreconcilable overlap of tram and church control.

This brings me to another point. When we do understand a culturally contingent joke, it takes on unbridled hilarity. Because we understand the reference, we feel extra good and often laugh louder and longer than usual to communicate our understanding and involvement in the culture. And that's no joke.

⊚ Honest Cheating

Cheaters never prosper, but at least they pass their exams.

Americans who teach in Poland are often frustrated by blatant cheating in the classroom: Polish students whisper across the room, exchange notes fearlessly and practically fall over their neighbors' papers for a peek. Geez, you'd think they'd at least try to hide it.

One Polish educator says "cheating is an industry" in the Polish classroom. A student described how high school girls wore *ściągawki* (cheat sheets) above their knees under their stockings. They crossed their legs and inched their skirts up for the answers during the exam. During an oral exam a university student cheated by peeking at a chart of technical information cupped in his palm. He was caught and severely dressed down by one of the examiners. A second examiner scolded him for his audacity: Most people cheat only on written exams.

And now—high-tech cheating. An American computer instructor was pleased with her university students' sudden curiosity for small fonts. Then she discovered they were just cramming info onto cheat sheets for exam time. She also saw how copyroom workers helped students by reducing copies of information down to little scraps.

Many students admit openly that cheating is widespread but shrug it off as a natural thing. One Polish student says that too much of the education in Poland is "nothing interesting, there's no satisfaction in reproducing information" so they cheat to pass. Some students say that they're required to learn excessive amounts of useless detailed information and "this system of teaching makes us cheat." For some, it's "friends helping each other" or insurance for a passing grade. A Polish student says that the higher the level of education, the less often people cheat. "I'm not proud of it but I've cheated," says a law student, "mainly in my first two years of study." Some exams are simply too difficult to pass without cheating, several students claim. One failed an exam in a subject she knew because she didn't cheat. When she retook the exam, she cheated and passed.

In other words, it's not dishonest to cheat, it's pragmatic. You'll find the same attitude in other European countries. Kind of like paying taxes in some places: You're a fool if you don't cheat.

One Polish educator explains cheating this way: "The school system is part of the government and there's nothing morally wrong with cheating the government." Someone who refuses to cheat might be considered an outsider or a goody two-shoes. So even clean-cut nerdy types will cheat or help their classmates. Since it's traditional to cheat, as one Pole says, you'll hear students brag and exchange cheating stories as if it's a sport. And then there's the attitude that if you can make a good cheat sheet then you know the material. You deserve to pass.

Polish teachers don't like cheating any better than the Americans. One Polish instructor, who is infuriated by cheating, caught a university student red-handed and sent her out of the exam room. "I felt really bad," he said, "I was wet with sweat, she was crying." He thinks that unclear policies on cheating and a reluctance among teachers to act as executioners result in some degree of tolerance. The Polish law student says students could have "problems" (failing the exam) depending on whether the teacher is "crazy" about cheating or more tolerant. At his school, punishment might be meted out to students caught cheating the second time.

The American computer instructor showed zero tolerance. To her students' surprise, she confiscated their cheat sheets during the exam. She says they had an awwww-c'mon attitude, as if she were unreasonable and uncooperative. "I don't know the stuff that well!" one student protested. Now that's an honest cheater.

⑨ A Fireside Chat about Money

I was wearing a new wool sweater and a Polish friend asked if I had bought it in the States. Yes. "How much did you pay?" she asked immediately.

Questions about the exact cost of new shoes, pieces of furniture or apartment rents surprise many Americans, but such discussions are not uncommon among Poles. Prices hold a special fascination because money and materialism have relatively new importance in Poland. In Communist days, the topic of precise sums wasn't very compelling; everything cost the same, no matter where you bought it. In these days of the market economy, prices vary. So instead of just where to find it, it's where to find it at that price. I think it's a good sign for Poland. (It's just too bad about all the *nouveau-riche* yuppies that come with the package of success.)

An American living in Poland for nearly two years revealed his acculturation to the Polish openness about prices. While admiring an American's spiffy briefcase, he found himself asking, "Oh, that's nice. How much did it cost?"

It does happen that Americans ask each other about the prices of things but the inquiry might be prefaced with, "I hope you don't mind my asking..." or "Can I ask you how much you paid?" to acknowledge that it is potentially private information. If the person feels uncomfortable giving the exact amount, the answer might be, "Not too much," "It was expensive," or "Don't ask."

Compared to Poles, Americans seem to have a sort of neurosis regarding how much something costs. There's the notion of if-you-have-to-ask-you-can't-afford-it as if we all should be too good, too comfortable, too secure to think or talk about money. There's an underlying belief that in social situations, the mention of money is vulgar; it exposes some kind of vulnerability. A successful, secure person of "a certain class," whatever that means, does not discuss money or the value of possessions except with close friends, if at all.

In the book *Class*, Paul Fussell depicts middle-class Americans as fraught with status anxiety. Paying compliments on possessions, he says, "is a middle-class convention, for this class needs the assurance compliments provide"—acknowledgement that they can afford nice things. However, asking the price is taking it a step too far. Fussell observes that among members of the upper class, "you have to refrain from uttering compliments, which are taken to be rude, possessions there being of course beautiful, expensive, and impressive, without question." That means I shouldn't walk into an opulent house and exclaim, "Hey, nice Ming vase. How much did that set you back?"

In any case, the Poles' discussions of possessions and their price tags do not necessarily indicate class but rather an adjustment to a new economy. These types of queries represent a cultural difference for most Americans—and yet it's tolerable. Maybe for some, it's even a relief.

When it comes to salaries, some Poles have a stereotype that Americans talk openly about their big fat paychecks. Not true—and in fact, many Americans might be surprised by Poles' frank conversations about earnings. If these discussions cause you discomfort, I recommend the strategy of describing your salary as *za mało* (too little), *za dużo* (too much), *wystarczająco* (enough) or just say *nie pytaj* (don't ask) and look depressed.

ⓢ Tips for the Unruly

In my own small way, I'd like to contribute to world order.

Here. Now. Before your very eyes. Let's talk about tipping in Poland.

Some time ago, at the Pułtusk castle, I was at a barbecue and bonfire by the river with a group of Poles. As we slurped beers and munched on kielbasa, a Polish folk band played. I wondered out loud if we needed to tip them. But none of my Polish companions could advise me if—and how much—to tip. "This is always an uncomfortable situation for Poles," one of them told me.

In the U.S., tipping may not always follow hard-and-fast rules but one thing is clear: If you don't tip, you're a cheapskate. So you tip waiters, waitresses, bartenders, bellhops, taxi drivers, room service, the parking valet, the hair stylist and pizza delivery man. In most cases, 15%-20% is a respectable neighborhood.

Until recent years in Poland, service gratuities weren't customary. When asked about current tipping habits, Warsaw waiters, waitresses, taxi drivers, bellhops and the pizza delivery man shrug and say the same thing—some folks tip, some don't. Poles aren't used to it and many West Europeans assume it's included in the bill. But a Polish waitress says when she's the customer, "I always tip 10%." Aha! We're finally getting somewhere. Other service-providers eventually arrived at the same figure after doing the it's-hard-to-say song and dance routine.

A Marriott employee tells me that restaurant wait staff salaries are set with the assumption they'll make some money off tips. Servers, however, don't know what kind of tips to expect. Any customer doubts are gently cleared up with a note at the bottom of each bill: "Gratuity at your discretion." This message is creeping onto bills in many restaurants.

The 10% neighborhood seems to be a safe one for restaurants but leaving less or nothing isn't the mammoth gaffe it is in the States. Just be aware that you will leave a disappointed service person behind. Of course, if the service resembles a crime, tip zip.

In taxis, tipping isn't obligatory either but it's appreciated. But if you want to tip, round up the fare and tell the driver what you want to pay. A few drivers say around 10% is common and one tells me that "Most passengers tip, even if it's just a little." However, the pizza delivery man said, "Sometimes Poles give some extra *groszy* and they think they're tipping. That's nothing for them and it's nothing for me." So there's a difference between rounding off for change-making and a gratuity. When they don't have small change, taxi drivers might round a fare down and they certainly aren't tipping you.

If you get your hair cut and don't look like a circus freak after a lawnmower accident, tip something. A gesture of any amount is appreciated though one hairdresser says she receives as much as 10%, mainly from her regular customers. Tipping for hotel bellhops also varies. At Hotel Europejski tips go "between five cents and ten dollars according to nationality." At the Marriott, an employee tells me around a dollar per suitcase is the average.

So back to my tipping dilemma with the folk band at the cookout: After a few beers, we decided we truly liked the music and debated the tip. We settled on buying the musicians some beers and they immediately took a break to drink them. They had obviously expected *something*. I breathed a sigh of relief. For us, world order was restored.

🌀 In Tune with Tone

I was buying some things at a fruit and vegetable stand. When I pulled my wallet out of my backpack slung over my shoulder, a bunch of *kabanosy* (dried sausages) slipped out, and fell onto the sidewalk. I didn't notice until I turned around and nearly stepped on dinner. "I'll give you a another bag for that," the vegetable man said, sounding a tad impatient. "No thanks, I live nearby," I answered. He insisted in an irritated tone, "I'll give you a bag. It'll be easier to carry!" The words were right but he sounded rude and bossy. It left me with an ambiguous taste in my mouth.

Word stress, rate of speech, loudness and intonation are subtle communication tools which can radically affect meaning. Intonation alone can make the word "wonderful" into an expression of delight or sarcasm. A person's use of pitch and stress can determine whether we walk away from a conversation satisfied or with the vague impression the other person was a jerk. And very often, the implications of voice are easily misinterpreted cross-culturally.

Employees at a major British airport complained that the Indian food servers in the staff cafeteria were "surly and uncooperative," and not polite like the British servers. Linguist John Gumperez identified intonation as the culprit. The Indians used a falling intonation when offering food, so an offer of gravy came out as a statement: "Gravy." As if to say, "This is gravy, take it or leave it." British servers used a rising intonation, "Gravy?" which sounds like a polite offer in English.

Polish intonation relies on a smaller range of intonation than American English so Americans might find Poles strangely cool or unenthusiastic at times. After returning from a tour in Canada, an actress friend described her experience there as *świetnie* (wonderful) with falling intonation. This made the trip sound more so-so than *świetnie*. But once she got rolling on her stories, I realized she really had had a fantastic time. My American ear just expected more rising and falling intonation to relay enthusiasm.

While Poles enjoy Americans' zeal, sometimes the American contours of intonation strike them as exaggerated or superficial. After spending some time in the U.S., some Poles had picked up the American style of expressing enthusiasm through pitch differences. One of their Polish colleagues observed, "They were saying 'Wow!' over small things like a new pen. They said it with this kind of voice that would have been okay for something really big, like if I were getting married." One Pole imitated American intonation (which sounded like squealing) and said, "Americans react like children. They sound infantile, but I like that." Gee, thanks.

There are some practical aspects to these differences in intonation. The director of a Warsaw dubbing studio says it's a struggle for Polish actors to dub over the voices of some American cartoon characters. An audition tape has to be sent back to the U.S. studio for approval so the Polish actors must try to recreate the cartoon character's original voice as closely as possible. Part of the difficulty, and the art, of matching the dubbed Polish voices to the original American ones lies in the different ranges of intonation between Polish and English.

Getting back to my vegetable man: When I mysteriously turned down his simple offer of a bag and he pushed a little harder to help, I realized the Polish way of helping is often at odds with the American value of self-sufficiency. But the issue here is that, while being kind, he relied on the kind of intonation an American associates with a command. A Pole may not find that very refined but wouldn't consider it impolite. I should have taken the bag saying with roller-coaster intonation, "Woooooow! Nice customer service!"

⑨ Mammal Message

Most people don't think about "kinesics," more popularly known as the study of body language, but they subconsciously register the paralinguistic signals of others. Naturally, the reading of another culture's body language is not always accurate. But it has an effect nonetheless.

Americans relay competence and trust to each other by standing straight with the shoulders back, the chin lifted slightly, a look of brightness in the eyes and a quasi-smile. Hand-gestures are used subtly. Americans sit with the torso leaned against the back of the chair and, men especially, extend their legs and drape their arms over chairbacks. This is the person with self-confidence, self-reliance—the one who gets hired, the one who earns a grandmother's trust. This overall physical stance says, "I know what I'm doing" and we try to convey a respectable first impression even if we don't deserve it.

Traditional Poles (mainly older ones) have a different style; rather than elicit respect, their demeanor conveys it. Expressing deference is always safer within a one-up-one-down system, and they do so with the head slightly lowered, shoulders somewhat rounded and facial expression serious. Hand gestures are made with the elbows close to the body. During conversation, very traditional Poles may even make a ducking motion with the head to communicate further modesty. To show attentiveness, Poles tend to perch on the edge of their seats, holding their extremities close to the body.

Unfortunately, those from the School of Chin-up-shoulders-back will interpret this type of deference-giving as timid or insecure. It won't impress an American employer who looks for a specific kind of "personal presentation" in an interview. Conversely, the American carriage might send a wrong signal to a Pole. It can send radar messages of arrogance and over-confidence to the Polish subconscious mind—a contribution to the stereotype of the imperious American.

People's body language can apparently be affected by how they view their social background. A study of immigrants to the U.S. in the 1920's showed that East European Jews gestured close to their sides, hunched their shoulders and shuffled their feet. This, of course, was related to their past of repression and persecution. The Italian immigrants' arm gestures, on the other hand (no pun intended), were predictably expansive and flowing, an expression of personal freedom. The more loyal these immigrants were to their ethnicity, the more they retained their groups' gestures over the years. Even their first-generation American children reflected their immigrant parents' body language. Ones who assimilated used more American-style gestures.

If such a phenomenon is universal, many young Poles are quickly adapting to and perhaps establishing the culture of the New and Improved Poland. Many seem to have developed new types of body language, depending less on the Polish deference-giving stance. I have noticed this especially among young Poles who work in foreign firms and university students who have spent time overseas; physically, they seem less Polish to me.

I haven't noticed if their sitting habits are any different from other Poles. Just for the record: Americans do not put their feet up on tables as much as people think, but interestingly, they do tend to occupy more space than Poles when sitting. This expansive seated posture resembles the behavior of dominant mammals who are known to take up more space than nondominant ones of the same species. As the Polish economy improves, God forbid that Poles start splaying themselves over the living-room furniture.

⑨ Smile Code

A Pole who has lived in the States for six years returned to Poland for a visit. During a round of introductions to some people in a cafe, she immediately spotted the American by his smile. "There's a lack of smiling here. It's not as spontaneous," says the Pole. Another Pole says, "Americans, in general, smile all the time. Here, people in the streets look worried."

Americans have the reputation of being friendly and approachable, and going around with a smile plastered on their faces may be a big part of why. But there is a Smile Code: A half or closed-mouth smile in the bank, store or bus serves as a courteous recognition of others' existence. It shows you are cooperative but not necessarily looking for social contact. A closed-mouthed smile—say, to an airplane seat partner—just might mean, "I'm a nice person but don't bug me, okay?" Big smiles are nice, but if you walk into public situations with a giant Cheshire cat grin, people might think you're crazy, stupid or on drugs. Or worse, a politician.

The broad toothy grin is the image mainstay of American politicians; it projects confidence and easy control to the point of cheesey cheerfulness. Clinton and Reagan were big grinners. Carter smiled a lot, almost too much for some people's taste. George Bush Sr. and George Bush Jr. seem to have a family problem: Their smiles look stressed with facial muscles pulling the mouth back rather than up.

By contrast, Polish political figures smile in public far less often. Former Prime Minister Waldemar Pawlak was a pathetic case in facial expressions. He was fulfilling the traditional Polish role—a good politician is a serious one—but he went too far. Polish politicians nowadays are far more media-savvy, like President Aleksander Kwaśniewski and Prime Minister Leszek Miller, but they still don't oversmile like their American counterparts. They know how to play their media cards right.

In everyday life, the approach to fleeting interactions in Poland is neutral or I-don't-care-about-you, so there are fewer smiles than Americans expect. Surface courtesy usually means a slight nod of the head (though I've noticed that younger Poles have started to use the cursory smile). And some Poles may not feel like masking their everyday preoccupations. From this perspective, the smile would be fake. In American culture, you don't advertise your daily headaches. It's bad form, so you turn up the corners of the mouth—or at least try—according to the Smile Code.

One Pole notes her compatriots' seriousness when they travel by train. Smiling at fellow passengers could be interpreted as a desire to

talk. The norm is to say *dzień dobry*, nod and look at them briefly as if to say, "I'm here, I see you, I don't want to disturb you." She says, "Maybe you can smile at a small child but not an old man or a guy of your own age—unless you want to seduce him." Hmmmm. But it's understandable; the smile is often an invitation to talk. And it's intensified by raising the eyebrows. In fact, a raising of the eyebrows alone serves the same purpose. Imagine looking across the room and seeing somebody lift their eyebrows at you. That's direct—from a stranger, even weird.

In any case, Americans smile more in situations where Poles tend not to, but this is changing. Poles are smiling more easily these days than they used to. The difference is that they just may not *initiate* an exchange of smiles in a quick or anonymous interaction, but they will react to a kind look. Okay, so you may see faces that might look serious or grumpy but don't jump to conclusions. Try a smile disarmament first—that's good politics.

◎ Socially Behind

Stand, shake, and turn. These three simple rules of body language are subtle but significant.

Perhaps I should explain.

Poles relay politeness and respect through discreet signals, which Americans don't use as a rule. Americans have a different set of signals which rely on informality—a type of social leveling, our own brand of politeness and respect.

The American tendency to lean towards the informal side in social relationships is one of our cultural strengths. But it can also be troublesome in cross-cultural situations. Americans recognize "proper ways" but pooh-pooh them if they involve formality or pomp. If a ritualized gesture appears stiff or unnecessary, we'll veer off onto the more informal route. This highlights our foreignness, which some Poles admire or just shrug off. Others judge more harshly and chalk it up to a lack of *savoir-vivre*.

So let's look at just three behaviors—stand, shake and turn—which Poles practice as a matter of etiquette:

Rule 1: Stand. In Poland, when you meet or greet someone, get off your duff and stand up. And, as a general rule, avoid sitting while talking to someone who is standing. This rule is relaxed for women but it's a Cretin Offense if a man sits and converses with a woman who is standing. If it's uncomfortable to stand—like at a table where coffee would get overturned—men especially should raise themselves a few centimeters off the chair for just a second. This gesture of standing even a little bit expresses respect.

When an American makes the motion to stand, the other American often says, "No, please don't get up." We actually prevent people from standing on our account.

Rule 2: Shake. Shake. Shake. Now I'm referring to hands. When arriving or leaving social or business situations, unless the situation is very informal or a big group is involved, Poles shake hands with everybody in the room. Move around the room whether leaving or arriving and shake everyone's hand. It doesn't matter if you're meeting new acquaintances or greeting familiar faces—just get movin' and shakin'. Shake paws with the dog if you feel like it. Then, do the same thing when you leave. In Poland, if you're sneaking out of a party, at least shake the hosts' hands. It's an offense not to do so in the States; it's a social felony in Poland.

Americans generally reserve handshakes for first-time introductions or business situations. In social situations, it varies; some shake, others don't. However, to most Americans, scooting around the room to shake everyone's hand appears stiff or—worse—politician-like. And when people do shake hands, it doesn't matter much who sticks the hand out first. In Poland, a woman usually extends her hand to a man, an elder extends the hand to a junior.

Rule 3; Turn, turn, turn. When you're squeezing by folks to get to your seat in the theater, think about where your backside is facing. Rear ends should face the stage or screen, not a person's face. You go to the opera and show your buns to the row of people's faces and you'll come off like an oaf.

I know, I know. People usually don't think about their behinds. But in cross-cultural situations, it's just safer to consider the end result.

73

⑨ One Touchy Subject

During a trip to the States, every so often a stranger would walk by me and for no apparent reason announce, "Excuse me," or "Sorry." This voice out of nowhere baffled me at first. Then I realized that folks were apologizing for coming too close to me. Hah! I hadn't even noticed. After all, I live in Poland, where strangers can brush against each other without a word.

A newcomer to Poland might be taken aback at the lack of space between strangers, especially while waiting in lines. Americans stand at least 18 to 24 inches from each other. Poles bunch up much more closely, almost touching or practically leaning on you. Maybe that crowded sense of urgency encourages people to take care of their business faster.

If you don't stand within breathing-down-neck distance in line, a fellow shopper might wriggle in. You get that old grade school instinct to yell out, "Hey! No cuts in line!" but then realize the person just got confused about whether you were in line or not. If you leave your two feet of American Stranger Space, someone might inquire, "*Pan(i) jest w kolejce?*" (Are you in line?)—a polite way of asking, "What's all this empty space doing here?" Or, if the person just steps in line in front of you, a gentle tap on the shoulder and *Przepraszam, ja stoję w kolejce* (Excuse me, I'm in line) will regain you your place.

How close you can get to someone is dictated by the social relationship. For Americans, the closest for regular friendly conversation seems to be about 18 to 20 inches. Any closer and you can bet there is intimacy in progress. The more formal and less familiar the relationship, the bigger the zone.

Some Americans are unnerved by the Polish casual conversation zone, which seems to be about two to four inches smaller than the American one—a short distance but enough to feel that creepy in-your-face effect which makes you pull back to the comfort zone. Which of course makes the other person lean in closer and has you feeling like conversational prey.

Then there's the touch issue. Some cultures favor more friendly tactile contact than others. In one study of cafe dwellers, Puerto Ricans touched each other an average of 180 times an hour, Parisians 110 times, and in London, no times at all. Touchy-feely experts say Americans are less inclined to express warmth through physical contact—we nudge, slap backs, give playful punches or squeeze an arm, but generally the contact is fleeting. When Poles really like you, you'll be rubbed, stroked and cooed over. Friends stroll arm-in-arm and Polish gentlemen offer women their guiding arms with ease. In the U.S., that kind of stuff is tricky between the sexes and can land you in court.

When someone offends our notion of space by standing too close or touching too much, notice that we never mention the infraction. We just correct the situation discreetly by moving away or stiffening up. Of course, you could say, "Excuse me, I'd feel more comfortable if you would back up about four inches while you talk to me and not touch me more than 60 times an hour." Then pull out a ruler and a stop watch. That will guarantee you lots of space.

⑨ A National Priority

Remember the American stereotype with the checkered jacket, mismatched pants and a cigar in his mouth? He died. But he has a replacement: the American schlepping around in a sweatshirt and sneakers with no socks.

Are Americans big slobs? Maybe. Some of us. But only on our days off.

Poles who visit the States sometimes comment on what bad dressers Americans are—jeans, old t-shirts, droopy jackets and baggy pants. Some Americans even putz around in public in their sweatsuits prompting some to tsk-tsk, "These Americans don't know how to dress."

But they do know how to dress—for comfort. They'll even pay a premium for clothes that are already worn-in and pre-washed. Comfort is a national priority especially during off-hours.

For parties, get-togethers or just on weekends, Americans tend to dress down more than Poles. And why not? They've been strangling in nylons and jewelry or a suit and tie all week so it's time to breathe easily in their favorite old sweater, broken-in khakis, and comfy shoes. More often than not this doesn't work in Poland; I've heard too many stories from Americans who showed up tragically underdressed for Polish parties. An evening out with Poles is usually a time for a little glamour and flash. And to show your hosts that your visit is something special. A young Polish couple working in the States blew a fortune on new clothes for their boss's party. They showed up at his house and were shocked to see the American guests in T-shirts and jeans. They found that disrespectful.

And notice at formal affairs or big theaters in Warsaw, you will see some pretty glitzy duds—the sequin quotient for fancy shindigs seems to be higher in Poland than in the States.

Americans go for comfort as often as possible. Some offices have their once-a-week "casual day" and there's even "corporate casual" and "casual chic." For walking to and from the office, women wear Reeboks with their business suits. And everyone knows that people who work for computer firms don't own suits. But when the dress code is in effect, it's strict. A Pole noticed that the idea of "the American uniform" for men is clear: "a dark suit, a white shirt and a loud tie." Women usually wear suits with skirts or pants or businessy-looking dresses. In either case, *le look américain* for the working set is generally understated and tasteful. Not flashy. Not distracting.

In Poland, there seems to be less of this uniform idea for work. Office garb varies widely, depending, of course, on where you look. It ranges from casual to flashy, sexy to conservative. In the slickest business offices, you might see men in suits, and women in huggy minis and high heels. On the whole, professional dress is simply less conservative and in some cases, less formal, less "put together" than what Americans expect.

Plus, note that many Poles are neatly dressed, though not necessarily elegant, when just out buying toothpaste or taking the kiddies to the park. The colors may not match but their clothes and shoes are well-cared for. It's terribly shameful to wear wrinkly, worn-out, frayed or holey clothes. That's how—eek!—a member of a lower class would dress. "Poles have a complex about that," says a Pole, "They'll even go out and buy new clothes they can't afford, to look like they have more money than they do—especially when they want to be dressed up." (Okay, but who doesn't go out and spend more than they're supposed to?)

In Poland, someone walking around in a broken-in pair of jeans and a sweatshirt might look like a student, someone on the way to fix the pipes or maybe an American. In the U.S., it could be anybody on a day off. I dress down on my days off and my Polish friend Robert sometimes comments on how I dress "young" or "in student style." He doesn't seem to understand I'm expressing my national priority.

⊚ Phoney Behavior

In the early 90's, phone use in Poland was as dependable as a teenager—moody lines and inexplicable breakdowns. "I couldn't get a hold of you" was a common excuse for no contact, and getting someone to take a message was asking for a big favor. Mobile phones? Hah!

In less than a decade, Poles joined the phone frenzy and there are addicts among them as in every developed country. Some carry more than one cell phone and pass their cell phone number out like candy. If business-intensive, they answer the phone with their name rather than saying *Hallo?* or *Słucham?* (literally, I'm listening). They return messages quickly and instead of smoking cigarettes, they habitually pull their phones out to check if they've missed a call or received a text message. They play phone tag a lot and judge their importance by how many messages they get when (if) they turn the ringer off during a meeting. The telephone is their life-line. In terms of mobile phones, Poland joined the EU a long time ago.

But because cell phones are still relatively new in Poland, proper behavior on how to use the technology hasn't fully developed. Too many Poles still boom out their conversations in stores, restaurants and on the street as if to say, "Look at me, listen to me! I'm important! Whoopee! I have a cell phone!" or they simply don't care that no one wants to hear their urgent conversations that usually go like this: "Hi, I'm in the store. Where are you? Okay. Bye!" However, among more cultured Poles, the idea of speaking quietly or leaving the area is taking hold, and signs designating "no phone zones" are appearing in restaurants and stores—evidence that new rules of behavior are emerging. Of course, rude people will continue to exist.

For foreigners, speaking Polish is already difficult and problems in another language are compounded on the phone. In Poland, it's important to follow a general rule of Polish phone etiquette by introducing yourself as the caller. Otherwise, you sound like the country bumpkin who's not used to telephones. For example, this is proper: *Dzień dobry. Dzwoni Aleksander Kwaśniewski. Czy mogę rozmawiać z Laurą?* (Hello. This is Aleksander Kwaśniewski calling. Can I speak with Laura?). The added benefit is that when Laura knows that Aleks is calling, she can mouth the words to the person who answered the phone, *Nie ma mnie!* (I'm not here!). If the person you're calling is in, you are asked, *Proszę chwileczkę poczekać* (Please wait a moment). If the person isn't there, the answer is *Nie ma go/jej* (He/she's not here).

Message taking is still a funny business in Poland. Many people won't offer to take a message so it's your responsibility to say, *Czy mogę zostawić wiadomość?* (Can I leave a message?). Don't be surprised if the person asks you to call back instead. Big or modern companies have voice mail systems or efficient receptionists but message-taking is still spotty. I recently asked to leave a message for someone at a multinational company and the receptionist said, "Oh, I don't know when I'll see him. Can you call back?" I insisted on leaving a message and she sighed, "Well, okay, I'll take it but I don't know when he'll get it." Not very modern of her but maybe she thought I was backwards for not having the guy's mobile phone number. At least I introduced myself.

Wrong numbers are just specks of electronic dust in the grand web of communication but Poles get their shorts twisted in knots over them. The recipient says in a huff, *Pomyłka*! (Wrong number!), as if you did it on purpose just to annoy them. Sometimes these calls can erupt into lengthy conversations; recipients act incredulous and ask detailed questions about numbers and names as if it's the *first* wrong number *ever* in Poland.

Anyway, when you make a phone call, you finish with a "closing sequence." You might repeat the reason for the call or say when you'll talk or see each other again. An exchange of words like "well," "okay" or "yeah" serve as last-minute checks that nothing else needs to be said. Poles say *no, dobra* (well, good) or *dobrze* (fine) and maybe *Nie chciałbym zabierać Ci czasu* (I don't want to take too much of your time)—this is ultra-polite for "I have to go now." Some say *Pozdrawiam* (Regards) or send regards to colleagues or family members: *Pozdrów Marka* (Regards to Marek). Less formally, Poles just say *No to część* or *No to pa* (Well, bye).

Notice that some people just won't let you say *do widzenia* (goodbye) by ignoring second or third closing signals. That's when you resort to gentle directness, "Well, I have to go now." Or in Polish, *Muszę już kończyć* (literally, I've got to finish already). If you need to say that, you're either dealing with someone who truly adores you or just a serious phone addict.

Your Work Life

ⓢ New Poles and Ambition

A Polish university student was agonizing over her choice of a major—finance or international relations—so I asked her which one she liked best. International relations by far, she told me; finance is boring. "Well, that's an easy choice, then, isn't it?" I asked. "No, it's not!" she said. "A degree in finance guarantees me a good job. I don't know what kind of work I can get with a degree in international relations." I asked if working in an area she found boring seemed attractive and she looked at me like I was a dunce, "But I'll work in a good company and make money." Hello, New Pole!

New Poles in business, career-driven in their mid-20's, are gung-ho on getting ahead. Foreign managers are often surprised by these young Poles' burning ambition; these career-driven Poles have seen too many people living in small apartments, working dead-end jobs and counting their groszy. They want a career, money and social status—a company car and cell phone don't hurt either. They think, "Hey, I'm smart and talented. I deserve that," and go out to get it.

This may seem unexceptional, especially to Americans, but just 20 years ago professional ambition in Poland amounted to getting a tolerable job when everybody was guaranteed work by the State; recognition for excellence was questionable and job satisfaction was a luxury. In the early to mid 90's Poles started to realize the personal payoffs of capitalism: nice salaries, benefits, challenging opportunities to develop and advance. Today, New Poles in business take such advantages for granted—evidence of a social transition cultured by an unbridled drive for success. They come to the workplace highly motivated, willing to work long hours, chomping at the bit for promotion: a manager's dream and a major force in the Polish business environment.

But more mature managers observe that a drawback is their impatience in getting ahead and unrealistic expectations. An Austrian who manages an international firm says that while young Poles are professionally ambitious, they don't yet realize that "they have to work for it and build it. They have short-term ambition but not long-term ambition. They'll change jobs for five hundred złoty more."

But look at their role models: Many of their Polish bosses aren't much older—in their mid- to late-30's—but hold prestigious and well-paid positions like Head of Marketing, Partner, Member of the Board or even President. Many of them happened to be in the right place at the right time; some were hired 10 to 15 years ago simply because they spoke English or were just available. In fact, some of these young Polish executives have non-business backgrounds with degrees in biology, geology, art history, philosophy or in one case, musicology. They learned quickly and hung in there. "We got spoiled," admits one of these high-fliers who marvels how at 40 years old he's often the oldest person in the room at his multinational firm.

But those days of being buoyed to the top are over. A Pole heading training and development for HR in a large multinational FMCG producer says, "Higher positions are filled and there's no longer such rapid growth. Companies find themselves stuck with young people with huge expectations, and these people suffer."

A Pole in his late 20's, a marketeer, has been bouncing between FMCG makers in Warsaw, searching for the best possibilities for advancement. "I was looking for the place where my talents would be recognized," he says. So far, he's disappointed: "It's not happening the way I thought it would."

And there are other new types of New Poles on the market too. Rather than high salaries and job status, they seek gratification and a chance to apply their education. A 23-year old about to graduate in law works in a restaurant. He plans to leave Poland for England where he'll work and save up money so he can afford to work as an intern back in Poland—this seems to be the only way for him to get professional experience. A twenty-four year old completed a degree in administration and a second in EU relations. She's applying for a job at a multinational firm but is unsure they need what she has to offer. "I don't want to be a manager. I want to do administration because I'm good at it. For now, I want experience at a decent job to pay my bills, and then I'll see where my talents take me."

These recent graduates' attitude differs from the money-driven student on the fence between her choices of a major, but they all have something in common: they're different from the Poles of the same age 20 years ago because they depend solely on themselves for their professional success. That's what makes them New Poles. Say hello.

⑨ Workplace Families

Why can't an office be more like a home? After all, work consumes much of our time, energy and soul. Some types of work just suck your blood directly—take a look at the pale, tired faces haunting the streets at the end of a workday.

The Polish attitude tempers some of this—the workplace should have at least some personal pleasures and comforts. "Poles like to turn the work environment into a home environment," observes a Pole. And indeed, they have a knack for creating a warm home-like atmosphere in the office. But if you're an expat outside the social loop, or experience cooperation as a slow-motion phenomenon, think about how you treat your workplace "family." It might explain why you're not flourishing the way you feel you should in the Polish workplace.

First, be aware of the Coo Factor. That is, Poles spend time cooing over their office family. That means highlighting mundane personal things, i.e. life: getting the brakes fixed, finding the right house paint and getting a kid to eat salad. It also means bringing someone coffee and noticing when a simple compliment is due.

On name days, (the Polish equivalent of a birthday), if you spot a cake, be proactively social: Stop for at least a moment, find out whose name day it is, say *wszystkiego najlepszego* (all the best). And if one of your Polish colleagues invites you to a party at home, pick yourself up and go. If you never accept or extend a personal invitation, you might as well pin a note to your chest, "Emotionally and socially unavailable." Because that's the message you're sending to Poles. If you want to show true commitment, have some drinks and speak heart-to-heart with your colleagues until the wee hours (but don't get sloppy).

Express a sincere interest in Poland. A Polish executive at an American multinational explains how her former American boss and mentor made a big impression on the Poles in their office: "He knew so much about Poland and its history."

Follow and ask about Polish current events that truly interest you. An English pal of mine is a big sports fan so he always has lots to chat about with the guys. He quickly tuned in to the fact that something like Adam Małysz's performance boosted the morning atmosphere around the office. One day his colleague was happy about how the Polish women's volleyball team performed in an international competition. "You're not interested in volleyball," he said to his buddy. "No," the guy admitted, "But it's good for Poland."

After you've established yourself, be more open—imperfect human that you are—by sharing some personal information about yourself. Confide simple things ("I can't do long division") or your dreams ("I'd like to run naked through Old Town"). Be revealing ("I feel guilty about that kid I pushed off the cliff when I was 12"). Talk about your spouse, your kids, your dog or your Venus flytrap ("It hasn't been eating lately. I'm worried").

And speak some Polish even if you think you're a big loser with languages (who doesn't when it comes to Polish?). Try out your crappy Polish in simple situations, like ordering in a restaurant, and ask your Polish colleagues for help afterwards if the waiter thought you were ordering an elephant instead of asking for a straw.

Sometimes, others' cooperation is linked closely to how personal you are with them (especially if dealing with government offices). That is, it may be their job to make copies, unlock the gate or process the shipping forms, but they might regard working fast as a favor. A young

85

secretary in a multinational admits she moves slowly in response to a colleague's requests since he rarely says good morning or talks to her.

A Polish executive says some situations call for "purposeful niceties." A Pole in sales at a medical supply company says his colleagues dole out his reimbursements faster since he took them flowers and chocolates on Women's Day. "I knew what I was doing. It was business," he says, "I think they like me and I need them." My English pal says it's important to be natural about it, not too obvious. One North American calls that "butt-kissing." Less cynical about the human spirit, I call it social skills.

In any case, extending extra special and personal attention to your colleagues is part of the Polish workplace "home"—you choose what kind of family member you want to be.

⑨ The Schmooze Department

Americans like to be get-to-the-point type of people when doing business—some small talk at the beginning of a meeting but don't waste time on frivolous chatter. Roll up your sleeves, plunge to the heart of matter and get the job done.

That's efficiency. Go team! Except that Americans and how they do business are the exceptions, not the rule, according to cross-cultural expert Dean Allen Foster. In *Bargaining Across Borders* he writes, "We Americans like to do business first and only then establish relationships. For much of the rest of the world, it has traditionally been the other way round: One must first establish relationships, and only then can we do business." Whoa! Americans weak in the Schmooze Department? Apparently so.

Americans are famous for their friendly small talk: weather-talk, forgettable chit-chat, innocuous conversation that gives people the chance to strut their social skills, relax a little and gather their thoughts before rolling up their sleeves. Poles have their own version and sometimes, for Americans, this talk might go on longer than expected for a business relationship—it might be more background information or more personal. One American says, "I like to get right down to business but I feel like I'm being rude if I don't talk about other things first."

In business relationships or "friendships" in Poland, you can ask favors of each other, bend the rules here and there, give special consideration to pals and socialize with your colleagues. This kind of expectations doesn't always sit well with Americans, especially early on in the relationship. Americans generally like to keep private lives and business lives separate so work associates making friend-like requests can be unsettling. Our behinds are uncomfortable on the fence between friendliness and friendship.

A Pole who deals regularly with government administrators and their offices says that "To do business, you should never talk about business. First show them that you're human, and then you can do

87

everything." This is The Grand Schmooze, heavy-duty stuff. Americans aren't used to that kind of relationship.

Further, showing your human side in Poland might involve getting schnockered at some point. Poland is certainly drifting away from its Eastern habits in many ways but *przeprowadzić sprawę przez bar* (to conduct business in the bar) still goes on in some places. Americans aren't used to that either.

But wait. A Polish executive in an advertising firm says that she simply does not have time for small talk or nights out. Last month, she had 55 projects in various stages of development going on at the same time. If someone called her up with chit-chat, she'd probably roll her eyes and cut the person short. She claims she's a bad example of business in Poland but she's actually a good example of the increasingly furious pace of work here. This can only mean one thing: Poland's Schmooze Department is being restructured.

⑨ A Terribly Good Job

Around 10 years ago the notion of feedback as a management tool arrived in Poland. Books, training and company guidelines have appeared instructing managers how to evaluate their employees' performance in a balanced, fair and helpful manner. One Polish executive trained to the teeth by an American corporation says, "If you understand the difference between critique and criticism, you're halfway there." That is, a critique includes the negative and positive and a good manager knows when and how to say both.

Polish managers now understand the importance of feedback but is it is used enough? "Giving balanced feedback is not typical Polish behavior," says an employee of a medium-sized American firm in Poland, "Companies are pushing it; regular meetings are advised but not all managers see it as adding value."

"Feedback is a very popular word" says a Polish HR specialist at an insurance firm, "but it's still not used regularly because people don't consider it a process."

It varies from company to company but shows us how the Polish mindset has changed in the last five years when feedback equalled criticism. A Pole working in a multinational firm says employees expect feedback and that "the new generation of young Poles who graduate from modern universities will ask for it directly."

Americans often use Sandwich and Cushion techniques for the critical part. Good bosses use these techniques consciously, others just do it naturally (when people do a good job by accident, we call them "talented"). For example, the negative part is sandwiched between sincerely positive remarks: "I like the structure of your report but it needs more details. I know when you focus on that, you'll do an excellent job." The Cushion might be a euphemism: An "area for improvement" might really be a weakness or it can put a spin on a comment. For example, a Pole and American were talking about some crummy evaluations. "The evaluations were really bad," the Pole said. "The evaluations were mixed with a shift toward the negative side," said the American.

All this warm fuzzy stuff is designed to evoke a reaction like "Hmmm, yes, I see what you're saying. Thank you for that constructive comment" rather than "Auuuugh! I'm a big loser!"

When I inquired about the problem—I mean, *the concern, the issue*—of criticism in the workplace, Poles said that Poles tend to take criticism on the job personally. That's understandable—if a manager doesn't practice good principles of feedback, the criticism might be very direct and harsh and may condemn a person's character rather than his or her behavior ("You're incompetent" vs. "I didn't get full information from you"). But even when a boss suggests to an employee that he needs to finish projects on schedule, there's a risk that the employee will interpret it as "I'm doing a crummy job, he hates me." The Sandwich technique is lost on Poles, says the Americanized Polish executive: "If a critique contains one little bit of negative, the Pole gets pissed off." Or, others say, the Pole hears only the positive part and shrugs the negative part off—if it's not direct, it's not serious. The point is that job appraisals, coaching and feedback are fairly new in Poland so reactions vary.

Personal relationships and a good atmosphere are very important in the workplace in Poland. So, some Poles say, sometimes it's just better if the negative goes unsaid. One Pole says that everyone in his office knows that the secretaries do a rotten job. But they all get along so fabulously, nobody dares say anything since it might shatter the great atmosphere. Another Pole says that things can get ugly because typically Poles get defensive and will cite reasons why the criticism isn't accurate ("Well, Piotr didn't give me all the right information"). One Polish boss says he's learned to avoid problems in his friendly office by prefacing criticism with "This is a professional remark, not a personal one..." That is, he stresses how he wants the person to change a behavior to do better and it's not an attack. That's a by-the-book feedback technique.

Not that the cushioning comments are meant to fool anyone; it simply shows good will by making the negative more palatable ("You're a nice guy and I'm sorry to fire you"). Americans easily accept this mix of negative and positive as a sign of respect. These days, the Polish workforce is so varied in age, education and amount of experience, they're far less predictable in their reaction to honest critiques. However, the ironic thing about Poles is that they're often very self-critical about how they accept criticism.

◎ The Buck Stops Here...or There

Depending on who you talk to in Poland, you'll find a big difference in how Poles take responsibility for their actions; it might be "the buck stops here" or "it stops over there somewhere."

In multinational companies, corporate culture demands personal responsibility – if you make a mistake, admit it, fix it or at least learn from it. Many companies formalize this type of expectation in their "competencies" (a document describing behaviors for success) so that employees know they have to be accountable. "A few years ago people didn't take responsibility," says a Polish employee with several years of experience in multinational companies, "but it's changed because of business. It's better that you admit your mistakes and learn from them instead of blaming others."

Great. But outside the royal gates of international business culture, responsibility shirking still lurks in Polish mentality. Before a training session started at a hotel, I saw that the room arrangement wasn't what we needed and asked for help in changing it. An employee launched into a long explanation of how he didn't know anything about it, so it wasn't his fault. The receptionist waved order forms in my face. "It's not our fault. Look at the instructions we got." I didn't care. I just wanted some help to change it.

The Polish director of a medium-sized clothing manufacturer and retail business says, "Polish people have guilty consciences. Sometimes I just want to discuss why something wasn't done, but employees feel accused and get defensive. This is very Polish."

When it comes to problems, some Poles place emphasis on deflecting blame and resort to explanations of external factors. It might involve pointing the finger at an entity ("It's the ministry's fault"), a situation ("Traffic was terrible") or someone else ("Jurek forgot"). This drives foreigners and Poles alike batty.

An American who runs a service company has 12 years of business experience in Poland. He says Polish employees used to blame each other but "have discovered that internal blame isn't so much fun, so now the game has evolved into blame-the-client for mess-ups."

I've observed that many Poles regard their own mistakes and shortcomings gravely. From early education onward, errors are viewed as something to avoid (as opposed to part of the learning process). Mistakes are reflections of your own inadequacies, evidence of your imperfections. You should know better, do better, be better. So it's important to clarify that something outside your power occurred, but that you're doing your job properly and competently. That way, you can't be criticized, punished or expected to take further action.

A few Poles theorize that dodging blame is a cultural remnant of Communist bureaucracy. Blame was passed from department to department, and it was never anybody's fault. Some shifty-eyed manager was always above you, telling you exactly what to do. If something went wrong, it meant that you didn't follow directions correctly. A black mark went on your record, or at least the incident wasn't easily forgotten – situations to avoid. In some cases, another Pole says, people would never admit to blunders since "mistakes could cost people their jobs." So the buck got passed around and around, and this mentality still exists in some places.

Americans have a different angle. One American sums it up this way: "It doesn't matter who made the mistake. There's an acceptance of the fact that there are problems." So, heck, if you muff up, admit and do something about it. There might be some grumbling and casting of glares around the room, but according to the values of American work culture, the important part is to move on and find a solution.

People who pass the buck are regarded as weaklings—an attitude you'll find only in the most enlightened Polish organizations.

So Americans know they should be buck-stoppers and take responsibility for mishaps and botch-ups. At least, that's the way we know we're *supposed* to act. But the important thing is to *act*. Pointing fingers is not acting, and when Americans experience Poles delving into long explanations of why-the-problem-isn't-my-fault, tempers simmer. After all, problems are inevitable. Or in the succinct words of American bumper-sticker philosophy, "Shit happens," so deal with it. The Polish version of that bumper sticker would read, "Shit happens and it's not my fault" (or, as the Polish saying goes, *Winni są dziennikarze i cykliści* ["It's the journalists' and cyclists' fault"]), meaning somebody else's fault.

A British senior director in a multinational company says, "I have never heard someone say 'I made cock-up', or 'We estimated wrong and were too early, too late in the market.' It's always the fault of the competition, the market, the client." But I also hear younger Poles and those with international experience sigh and cluck over the shame of people who are buck-passers. So if you hear a Pole say, "I made a mistake and will deal with it," or "Not my fault! Not my fault!," you'll know if you're dealing with modernized Poland or a bit of unfortunate history.

⑨ Sweaty Salesmanship

A friend wrote me about his recent professional accomplishments: "My hugeness is exceeded only by my vastness." While I found that funny, a Pole would most likely find it distasteful.

Tooting your own horn is firmly grounded in the American mentality—we've been conditioned to "sell ourselves" and behave confidently even when we're not. That's partially why Europeans consider Americans arrogant: too heavy on the confidence, too light on the modesty.

The more you are around Poles, the more you will be struck by their propensity for modesty—and charmed by it. After an incredible multi-course dinner prepared by a Polish friend, I told her how her cooking talents amazed me. "Oh, well, you know, a bored suburban housewife," she said with a smile. A Pole explained how he landed a big contract for his company: "I lucked out," he said though I knew he had worked hard on it. A Pole working in advertising sums up my favorite thing about Poles (and people in general): "Modesty is a good tone and sign of refinement. You don't have to say certain things—it should be obvious so you don't have to sell."

There is a group of young Poles called *pampersi,* known for their annoying arrogance, but traditional Polish thinking was that no one

person should be better than the next, and people would quell any talk of superiority or exceptional talents. Polish sociolinguist Adam Jaworski says that modesty is highly valued in Polish culture, and points to differences in American and Polish self-presentation. The American way ("Listen to what I did") is "confirmation-seeking"—listeners agree with the speaker and offer congratulations. This sounds arrogant compared to the dripping-with-modesty Polish style ("I'm not very good..."). Jaworski calls this "elicitation"—listeners contradict the understatement and offer praise. Jaworski says both ways serve the same function: seeking recognition and confirmation of self-worth.

Only in the last few years have Poles been living with the necessity of the self-sell: Western influences invaded the Polish workplace at breakneck speed, and Poles have changed their attitudes about how to present themselves, land a job and get some recognition.

Modesty is still admired in Polish culture but Poles realize there are times to dispose of it. Consider the Polish proverb *Pokorne cielę dwie matki ssie* (The quiet calf can suckle two mothers). Everybody admires that quiet, determined calf who accomplishes much. But when that little calf goes in for a job interview, he now bleats loudly—something Poles are getting comfortable with.

HR specialists and recruiters have witnessed improvements in the Polish self-sell over the past years but ambiguities and problems still exist. "Poles with experience in multinationals don't have a problem with selling themselves," says a Pole in her early 30's who recruits for a large Polish company, "There's big room for improvement with others." For example, at her company, candidates are very modest and undersell themselves. But an HR specialist at a multinational FMCG producer says "The labor market is tougher so people have to oversell themselves in the CV." But then the interview might tell the real story. For example, a Pole working in television saw how a job applicant described herself as computer-literate but didn't seem familiar with simple functions. An HR person tells how a job candidate responded to the interview question, "How did you learn from a mistake you made?" "I haven't made any mistakes," replied the candidate. A Polish lawyer says that job applicants at law firms always say that they are great.

A British senior director at a multinational says, "Candidates think they're playing the game but they're not. They're uncomfortable so they oversell and don't let their personalities come through" He says that, "During an interview, one guy looked me in the eyes so intensely—obviously using a technique he had learned—I was relieved when he left."

Okay, so some people exaggerate to get their foot in the door. Unfortunately this is normal in a competitive market and the most ambitious Poles in their 20's realize it. "The best candidates are the ones who know how to talk about their qualifications but show that they are still Polish," says a Pole working in recruitment. Still Polish? What does that mean? "That they are human." Amen.

⑨ Work vs. Real Life

When I lived in the States, I used to think I was funny when I would roll my eyes in mock exasperation and say, "Oh, I just *hate* it when my work interferes with my social life!" Ha ha! As if social life could be more important than work.

No way—not when Americans "live to work," according to cross-cultural expert Dean Allen Foster in *Bargaining Across Borders*. Yes, working is our *raison d'tre*. Poles, on the other hand, "work to live," says Iwona Benoit, a young Polish scholar who completed a study on Polish and American work values. For Poles, work is necessary but not the center of existence. However, Benoit notes, Polish professional and personal values are also changing.

For Americans, the personal and the professional should be kept separate. A conventional belief is that you don't do business with friends and family. And work always comes first. Ideally, personal calls, errands and matters go undercover at the office. And when you can't get together with your friends, there's no need to explain beyond that one magic word: work.

Poles value a balance between professional and personal lives; working too much draws pity from friends and self-pity as well. "When your excuse for not getting together with friends is that you're still at work, it's a real shame," says a Pole. Sometimes, the professional and personal might even overlap—it's perfectly natural (or even necessary) to do business with friends and family.

In Poland it's natural to experience a rich social life with work colleagues. For Poles, work relationships can get very personal, involving more intimacy than the surface courtesy Americans are known for. According to Benoit, Poles try to build an "affectionate atmosphere" in the workplace while Americans place "relative unimportance" on personal relationships at work. In other words, Americans may be open and friendly but the bottom line is business. A British senior manager working in Poland and other Central European countries says his view is similar, and he's heard from his colleagues that they wish he would spend more time talking to them about their personal lives.

The idea of personalizing work relationships is echoed by a Pole who developed his professional career in the States. Now in Poland, he says he goes out of his way to be on excessively chummy terms with his Polish colleagues. In his mind, it's just the way to be, and he's well-liked in his office. Besides, when he wants computer service, a report or slides printed, it's done. "To be formal means problems," he says. In other words, things *might* get done more for personal reasons than professional ones.

As most foreigners quickly realize, family life in Poland is front and center. This personal side of life competes with work from time to time—a family event can be a legitimate excuse to duck out of the office early. Or to change jobs. Many working women manage to arrange their schedules according to their children's school schedules. The point is, for Poles it's natural that their personal life—their family life—influences their work life. Poles are very European in their regard for work: It's not the be-all-end-all of life as it is for many career-driven Americans.

This is changing, mainly in urban areas, but it doesn't mean that Poles are happy about it. Take a look at Warsaw these days, where the workhorse disease has spread: Poles work such long hours that they're shocked themselves. For many, their personal and family lives take a back seat to work. A Polish mother arranged her kid's birthday party by phone while on a business trip outside Poland; a Polish businessman complains he's missing his kids' childhood.

Choosing work over personal life is second nature for Americans, though they have become concerned recently with the notion of work-life balance. For Poles it's not a question of finding that balance, it's a question of preserving it.

Polish Specifics

⦿ The Age Box

Okay, okay. So it's not the pinnacle of politeness to ask people how old they are. But in my mind, if you're comfortable with someone it's permissible. Feeling this golden moment had arrived with a Polish acquaintance of my age, I asked. She got a bit huffy, as if I had asked her if she drooled in her sleep.

Age reveals far more personal information about Poles than Americans (for our purposes here, let's put aside that traditional no-no of asking women their age). In Poland, age places people in distinct boxes of development and responsibility. In other words, social expectations are pretty clear—and that's typical of traditional societies. By contrast, Americans often ignore or break barriers and stereotypes created by age: Eternal youth isn't such an outlandish goal.

"There isn't the idea of 'you're as young as you feel' in Poland," says a Pole who lived in the States, "It's more like, 'you're as old as everyone else your age.'"

Another Pole describes aging in stages of "shoulds": "When you're in your early 20's, you should get a job. Then, you should get married and have kids so you're responsible for other people. When you turn 30, you should have total stability." Those who don't toe the age line are cause for concern: A 25-year-old Polish-American says according to her family, she's inching toward "old maid" territory; a 27-year-old man without a girlfriend is an "old bachelor." After a few years of marriage, childless couples draw curiosity, suspicion or pity. But this represents flack from their families—more modern Poles marry later than their traditional families might expect. A 32-year-old professional woman says her career and independence are most important to her right now.

So to some extent those age boxes are changing, but youth gets fettered in another way these days. In cities, witness the young Poles holding jobs with hefty titles like "manager" or "director." And that's a concern in the upper echelons of multinationals—how will these whipper-snappers handle the responsibility? Well, usually with a bit more stormy weather and a little less leadership aplomb. But they're willing and able—they just take an extra deep breath before their plunge.

When I was teaching at the university, I found a last-semester student hanging his head over his glass of tea in the student buffet. "What's wrong?" I asked, figuring he had failed an exam or was about to. "Life is going too quickly," he shook his head, "I feel old."

He was 23, about to step into a new box.

I guess I could have told him to get plastic surgery, enroll in an exercise class, take up a hobby, and use Grecian Formula, Rogaine, Botox and the face-a-cizer which builds face muscles and reduces wrinkles. But then I remembered, youth-a-cizing isn't the raging industry in Poland yet like it is in the States, where the search for long-lasting youth has blurred the lines of our age boxes.

In fact people who don't "act their age" are often cheered on by Americans. It's part of our we-love-diversity mentality. One American says, "When Americans see an old man rollerblading, they say 'Hurrah!' Poles would point and say, *'Wariat'* (lunatic)." She complains passionately, "In Poland, at a certain age, there's pressure to act like an adult. You're not allowed to act goofy." She probably speaks from experience—she's 34 years old and likes to act goofy.

Anyway, I tried to cheer up that student in the buffet—you know, show him life's not so bad after 23. After all, at my age, I wasn't decrepit yet. So I told him my age and he looked up at me to say, "Oh. I'm so sorry."

⑨ Family Ties

One night, I invited a colleague to join me and some pals for a beer. He said he'd show up late. His father was staying with him so he wouldn't go out until his father went to bed. *Until his father went to bed?* What kind of cockamamie excuse is that for not spending time with the gang? Another time, I told him that I would call him the next day. "Okay," he said, "but call before five. That's when my mother is coming to visit." This guy was 31 years old. Was he a momma's boy?

Absolutely not. He's an adult son who actually spends time with his parents. This is one of the requirements to be a Pole. However, it's getting tougher these days in Poland because the country is becoming more mobile and family contact is starting to change.

In America's society-on-wheels, there's nothing unusual about not seeing your parents or adult siblings much during the year. It doesn't mean you don't care; you just have your own life but stay in touch by phone, maybe see each other on special holidays. That's just the way it goes in a country where it's common to live thousands of miles away from family members.

In Poland, traditional family life—extended family life—continues no matter what age the kids are. Weekends mean Sunday lunches with grandparents, aunts, uncles, cousins, in-laws and kids galore. Or if they live *really* far away it means a weekend visit though less often than traditional Poles would like. An American spent the weekend in the country with a Polish family. The 40-year-old son misbehaved and caught hell from his kid and 100-year-old great-grandmother who called his aunt over to yell at him. A weekend family gathering like that in the States would probably make it into the local newspaper.

Polish parents expect to stay involved in their adult children's lives throughout life. Parents of adult children need to be needed and feel cut out of the action if they're not. Some Polish parents were hurt and confused when their daughter and Norwegian son-in-law refused their gift of a huge apartment in their same apartment building. The couple just didn't want to live under their noses, and that caused tension in the family.

Parents help young couples get started in life by helping out financially and with decision-making. Then as grandparents, they expect to stay involved by taking care of the grandkids—if they live in the same city. Just take a walk in the park on a weekday afternoon and see who's pushing the strollers and buying the ice cream. Then, when Gramps and Grannie are old and decrepit, their children take care of them and that might even mean living together.

And living together, from an American point of view, is the colossal disadvantage or impracticability of this great family system. Independence for the nuclear family is important and natural. We usually don't live with our parents and don't depend on them to take care of our kids because they live far away. There a lot of lost older souls far from their families but many do find satisfying ways to enjoy their old age. An American points out that there are typical "old people's hobbies" (like bird-watching, stamp-collecting, mall-walking, bingo or bridge) that don't involve babysitting and cooking. Some get involved in the community, socialize and travel. Some live in retirement communities with assisted-care and medical support if they're frail. Poles find this odd because retirement homes are not communities in Poland.

But they might start changing their views soon. Because of growing social mobility, a lot of unsatisfied elderly people are missing their traditional role in the family. They're struggling with the changes in Poland that affect their lives and those of their adult children. Let's see how the Poles handle their dedication to their parents.

⓽ Meet the Cast

There are certain "types" in everyday Polish life that you might see or hear about—the cast of characters who make up the Variety Society Show. To understand their images—and social implications—here are some of the stereotypes often referred to in conversation:

Matka Polka: Symbol of the all-giving homemaker, backbone and support of the Polish family. A professional mother, she is lord and master of the home. She is selfless and strong and would kill to protect her family. Purveyor of tradition, she leads the family to church every Sunday. She cooks, she cleans and tends to every family member's needs. Her arms stretch to the ground carrying grocery bags with a child at each hand. She's well respected but is a dying breed in big cities. (positive term, also used ironically)

Dystyngowany Pan and *Prawdziwa Dama:* This couple represents Old World grace and sophistication. Educated and knowledgeable, they inspire respect wherever they go. They listen to you attentively and then make connections between your blabber and the work of great writers and artists. They're unflappable and emanate inner peace. He always kisses women's hands, she defines grace. Both are dressed tastefully whatever the occasion. You delight in their company. (positive)

The Biurwa: From the word *biuro* (office) and a Polish vulgarity. She's the ill-mannered office worker who prevents you from doing whatever it is that you want to do. Between drags on her cigarette, she tells you she can't accept your documents due to a spelling error: "Next please..." You hate her. (negative, vulgar)

The Dziad: An old fart. Grumpy. Scolds people in public. Could also be an old bum. (negative)

The Stara Baba: The strong heavy woman who often sells flowers from buckets or garlic on the street. She's had a tough life but barrels on. She's on a pension. She wears a scarf on her head. Don't mess with her. (negative)

The Cieć: The doorman or building caretaker. He's your protector, best friend or pain in the butt depending on why you draw his attention. (neutral)

The Handlarz: The street peddler who sells anything from sweaters to watches to pumice stones off a card table or a cloth spread on the ground. Easterners often play this role; identify them by the huge striped plastic bags they drag around during off-hours. They usually wear plastic flip-flops and sweatpants in the summer; a beat-up ski-jacket in the winter. (neutral or negative)

The Krawaciarz: This person earns big bucks at sleek high-powered offices. Driven and dependable, they carry the latest mobile phone and electronic organizers. They're never "quite there" when you talk about anything but business. They're impeccably dressed with perfect hair. They look important whether they are or not. (slightly negative)

Pampersi: People in their late 20's to early 30's, have been promoted a bit beyond their abilities but still think they know much more than they do. Exude self-confidence and tirefully arrogant. Consider modesty a weakness. (negative)

The Żul: The tough who commits petty crimes. Swiper of car radios and wallets. Often spotted wearing jean-jackets. Hangs out a lot and smokes cigarettes. (negative)

The Pinda: The overdressed bitch, thinks she deserves to be adored because she wears spike heels, short skirts, black stockings and a lot of make-up. Looks like she's on an eternal trek to a night club. (negative, almost vulgar)

The Robol: The worker in overalls. Often looks like he just rolled out of bed. Extra friendly after drinking lunch. (neutral)

The Szyja, Łysy or Dresiarz: Meets with people at night clubs to do business. Wears thick gold jewelry, expensive leather jackets and jeans or sport pants. He's heavily built, thick-necked like a weightlifter. Hits people over the head with bottles when irritated, drives a car with tinted windows. (negative)

⑨ Tongueless Talk

One common way to check whether you are human or animal is to test your ability to use a formal and complex language system. Man can speak; our friends the primates cannot. In fact, some scholars say that "homo loquens" (speaking man) is the most appropriate name for our species.

In spite of our lofty *homo loquens* status, we often regress to our pre-language Neanderthal state and resort to gestures. This can be a real advantage if you find those streams of Polish consonant clusters daunting. Of course, communication with Poles will be limited, but at least efficient and clear.

To help develop your physical savvy, here's a brief lesson on common Polish gestures:

1. To wish someone good luck, hold up your fists with your thumb concealed within. Poles often add *Trzymam za ciebie kciuki* (I'm holding my thumbs for you). This is the equivalent of crossing your fingers.

2. If you wish to show approval of something or someone, you bend your arm, stick your elbow out and make a fist at chest level. This is like giving the thumbs-up endorsement.

3. To express frustrated anger, you show *żyła* (vein) or, in slang, *gula* (a swollen ball)—an imitation of a pulsing vein ready to pop with aggravation. Act as though you're holding a baseball up to the side of your neck. For extra special effect, make a noise like "gongggg."

4. When you want to show that something or someone is loony, tap the middle of your forehead with your index finger—*puknij się w czoło* (knock to the forehead). North Americans usually do it by swirling the finger at the temple.

5. To indicate that someone is drunk, make a chopping motion with your hand to the side of your neck. To communicate drinking in general, lean your head back, make an "0" with your mouth, and flick your finger several times against the area under your chin. If you do it correctly, it will produce a *mamrotek:* the glug-glug sound made when you pour vodka out of a freshly opened bottle.

6. To relay "I don't believe a word you're saying," take a forefinger and tug down the lower eyelid. The optional comment is *Jedzie mi tu czołg?* (Is there a tank driving in my eye?). The smart-alecky answer is, *Tak, i strzela* (Yeah, and it's shooting).

7. A gesture to indicate that someone can *załatwić* (arrange) something in an illicit way is a wiggly snaking motion with the hand, palm perpendicular to the floor.

8. For a situation in which nothing will be given or nothing was gotten, convey "zero" by showing a fist with the tip of the thumb sticking out between the index and middle fingers. This represents a *figa* (a fig), a fruit that used to be so rare and exotic in Poland that nobody ever actually saw it.

9. The well-known but less vulgar European equivalent of holding up the middle finger is: Make a fist, grab the inside of the elbow with the other hand, fling the fist upward, and stop it suddenly at about face level. This is known as the *gest Kozakiewicza*, named after the Polish Olympic pole-vaulter who was greeted with aggressive boos and hisses by the Russians at the 1980 Olympics in Moscow. After making the jump that earned him a gold medal, he landed, turned to the Russian spectators, and made this rude gesture. On live TV.

10. This vulgar one ranks high on the Scale of Obscene Insults and is for men only: Gesture as if you are shading your privates from the sun with your hand at angle, palm down. Sticking out the thumb palm-side is optional. Prepare for a fist fight if you use it on a Pole.

Note: Before you use any of these gestures, I'd advise a practice session on Polish friends for confirmation of your physical accuracy. Otherwise you'll just wind up looking like an uncoordinated Neanderthal rather than a sophisticated one.

⑨ Saint Garlic

There I was, sitting out in the country with Polish friends and relatives. Or *trying* to sit—my back was out of whack. "I slept strangely," I said to explain my Frankenstein-style walk. "That's from a draft that blew on your back," somebody said. "The nerves in your back caught a cold." "You should stay out of the cold." "Dangle from a tree branch." "Take vitamin B12." "Tie a woolen scarf around yourself," "Cat fur helps. Have a cat lie on your back." Hmmm, but I'm allergic to cats—how about a few hamsters? "No, it has to be *cat* fur."

You know how it is when you mention a health problem: free advice from anyone within earshot. Americans will recommend their favorite physician or pill and leave home medicine to the earthy-crunchy crowd. But in Poland (and most of Europe), people who don't even wear Birkenstocks practice home remedies regularly.

For colds and flus, Poles go for the gusto—they go for the garlic: raw, mixed in hot milk (which supposedly prevents you from smelling like a walking salad). And guess what? *The Doctors' Book of Home Remedies* published by *Prevention Magazine* says that "garlic is one of the best natural antibiotics and antiseptics." Poles swear by the powers of St. Garlic.

At the first sign of a cold or sore throat, the classic Polish treatment is vodka with lots of pepper. A few weeks ago, a Pole on a camping trip downed this taste-treat when she felt a little ill. The most significant result was she "had a red face and couldn't breathe for ten minutes." But besides that, she didn't get sick. Poles also recommend warmed spirits with honey or burnt sugar. After the alcohol treatments, you're supposed to go to bed and sweat out impurities. Some people even rub themselves down with spirits for extra warmth.

For full-blown colds, Poles, like everybody else, go for chicken soup. And get this: *The Doctors' Book* quotes researchers who found that chicken soup "appears to possess an additional substance for increasing the flow of nasal mucus." That means—yay!—extra nose-blowing to remove germs from your body.

Poles fanatically avoid bodily contact with any type of cold temperatures to stave off illness (it's "temperature phobia," says an American). If you walk around your house without slippers, you're obviously crazy. Don't cram drinks with ice like the wacko Americans—cold drinks cause sore throats or make them worse, they say. Eating ice cream with a sore throat reveals suicidal tendencies. And, you must keep your neck covered with a scarf AT ALL TIMES. Poles of all ages will tell you to wear a scarf to bed. And don't forget your hat to protect your ears from the evil, evil wind.

For rheumatism or arthritis: Sit on an anthill and let the ants bite you. Their poison stimulates circulation and relieves stiffness (yes, and who wouldn't jump and run?). If for some reason that remedy doesn't appeal to you, tie some cabbage leaves around your limbs. Or whip yourself with the branches of some stinging nettle. Added bonus: You might be forgiven for your sins.

To treat any type of virus: Leeches will suck impurities out of your body (and you thought your job was bad). Okay, so nobody really does that today. Instead, find somebody to do *bańki* (jars or cupping), an ancient but still-used treatment. Glass jars are attached to your back by suction (air is either sucked from the jar by a flame or a syringe) and the sucking effect stimulates the immune system with the increased blood flow. It's similar to the effect of leeches but it's not as much fun. Of course, if that doesn't work, there's always St. Garlic.

⑨ Name of the Day

Everyone deserves some special attention sometime. That's when birthdays come in handy. But after a while, you don't *want* attention just because you're getting older.

Polish custom to the rescue: Instead of birthday hoopla, Poles celebrate a person's existence by way of the "name day" (*imieniny*). All names in Polish (most of which are from saints) have a day: for example, Ewa's Day is December 24, Lech's Day is August 12, Tomek has seven name days in the year and Marek, eight. Maria takes the cake with a whopping 25 days. When parents give their child a name celebrated more than one day, they usually choose the closest upcoming name day. Even nerdy names get a day: Rufina's Day is July 10, Egbert's Day February 24 and Scholastyk's Day is February 10.

The best way to celebrate a friend's name day is a party with lots of food, alcohol, presents and flowers. Of course, everyone sings a round of *Sto Lat*—the song of "100 Years" as in "may you live 'em." (The lyrics are slightly more profound than the Happy Birthday ones). The guest of honor stubs a toe at the ground and says something like "Aw shucks."

The name day stops at nothing so you'll see a fair amount of it at the office. But here's the catch: The person who has the name day is obligated to provide the gala goodies (cakes, coffee, champagne, etc). Office cohorts *expect* it. In turn, they'll supply the kisses and wishes. Maybe gifts.

The Polish name day celebration is a tradition so pervasive, so unstoppable, it has the power to close down a whole company for a day. Take Michał's Day for example. Everyone knows a Michał. Employees might be celebrating the name day of five Michałs in five different departments. Of course there'd be inter-department revelry and pretty soon nobody's answering the phone, reading e-mail or returning phone calls.

I don't mean to be an alarmist here. I'm just trying to make a point. The name day is not to be tinkered with. It's a strong tradition.

Remembering the day is a litmus test of friendship and traditional types might expect you'll show up without an invitation.

Some folks have extra famous name days. April 23 is Jerzy's and Wojciech's day—two popular names so everyone expects to celebrate with at least one of them. People remember Barbara's Day, December 4, since *Barbara po lodzie, Boze Narodzenie po wodzie* (Barbara on ice, Christmas on water, meaning a cold Barbara's Day means a warm Christmas day and vice versa). *Andrzejki,* the eve of Andrzej's day, November 30, is the time of fortune-telling by pouring wax. On Marzena's day, April 26, Poles mark the first day of spring by tossing a dummy into the river.

Think of the advantages of a name day over a birthday. Birthdays are easy to forget; name days are obvious. If your friend is Małgorzata, all you have to do is ask her in which month she celebrates: January, February, April, July, October or November and look up the date on a Polish calendar.

So now you want a name day too—where do you sign up? Well, here's some privileged information on how foreigners can acquire their very own name day. Get a calendar and find the Polish version of your name. (If it exists. If you're Buffy, Trixie or Big Dada, don't bother.) On your special day, just announce that it's your name day and pull out a bottle of wine and a cake. Or just throw yourself a party. Nobody will question it. And the best part is nobody will ask you how old you are.

◎ Your Lucky Day

Breaking mirrors, walking under ladders and crossing paths with a black cat. Hah! What silly superstitions. We really don't take them seriously, right? Well, except that high-rise hotels skip 13 when numbering their floors and airlines find flights on Friday the 13th less full than on other days.

In Poland, there are more superstitions than people can keep track of. Some of these old beliefs vary from person to person, some are just obscure.

One of the better known superstitions in Poland is that if you see one nun, it's bad luck. Two nuns are good luck. I wonder, then, if nuns feel guilty when they have to go out somewhere alone. Another common superstition is that it's bad for a relationship if you shake hands across a threshold—you should step out or invite the person in. This has even evolved into a matter of politeness in Poland. And if someone wishes you good luck, it's bad luck to answer "thank you." If you wish someone good luck, say at exam time, they often respond, "I don't say thank you."

Seeing a chimneysweep is good luck, but in Poland don't forget to hang on to your shirt button. Some say to hold it until you see a man with glasses while counting backwards from ten.

According to a Russian superstition adopted by Poles, if you leave your house, and then return for something you forgot, you must sit down for a moment. If you don't, your trip will be bad or your day ruined. "I'll always sit down for minute," admits a Polish-Russian friend. His life is going fine so it must be true.

If you drop a utensil from the table, *Ktoś się śpieszy* (someone's in a hurry) meaning that someone's in a hurry to see you. If it's a spoon, it's a woman; a knife (or a fork) means a man. Also at the table, if you eat something for the first time, someone should pull your ear for good luck. For the first vegetable or fruit of the season, somebody hits the others over the head with a spoon. Beware during berry season.

There's also an Itchy Category. If your nose itches, you're going to be angry. One variation says that an itch on the right means you're going to argue with someone. On the left it means that love and sex are coming your way. If your right palm itches, you'll meet someone new but an itchy left hand means you'll get some money. However, a *single* person has to scratch your hand to make these things come true. Maybe it's a good pick-up line: "Excuse me, could you scratch my hand? Do you come here often?"

At a business function, I gestured for a young Polish woman to pull her chair closer next to me at the table. She refused, explaining that she'd have to sit at the corner—for an unmarried woman, it would mean she'd never get married. Women should also avoid putting purses on the floor since "money will walk away" as a Polish woman was recently told at her dentist's office. Lighting your cigarette from a candle is bad luck or it means that a sailor is drowning. Chainsmokers drown boatloads, a Pole notes.

If you misbutton your shirt so it's crooked or put it on inside out, either you'll have bad luck that day or you'll get drunk. In either case, common sense says you'll look like a big goof.

Then there's the Sneeze Before Breakfast Series. On Monday, the sneeze means something exciting is going to happen. On Friday, it's bad luck. On Saturday, it means plans for Sunday won't work out or someone's going to die. The Sunday sneeze means someone likes you.

117

Of course, superstitions are just irrational but beloved little rituals and habits. Nothing terrible will ever happen to us because of sneezes, itches or nuns. Knock on wood.

⑨ Blooming Protocol

Flowers are a biggie in Poland. And there all kinds of occasions and non-occasions to give them. If the *Kwiaty Non-stop* (24 hour flower mart) in Warsaw is any indication, you can give flowers just about anytime.

A bunch of blossoms is especially appropriate when you are visiting someone at home for the first time or even greeting arrivals at the airport or train station. And naturally, birthdays, name days, holidays and anniversaries are protocol screams for flowers.

The color of flowers isn't as important as it once was. Just about any color will do though white is associated with weddings or funerals. Flowers in a country's colors can be used in official bouquets but this diplomatic tradition seems to be on the wane. A Polish family remembers when yellow flowers signaled a man's open jealousy, and pink was a "safe" color to give, especially to old ladies. Only the romantic meaning of the red rose seems to have survived.

It's always better to buy flowers for acquaintances or celebrations, but hand-picked flowers will charm close friends—just have the decency to brush the dirt off the roots.

In many countries there's one flower which—if you buy it—exposes you as a dumb foreigner. In Poland the big no-no flowers are chrysanthemums and lilies, appropriate only for funerals. So don't show up for dinner implying that the outing is social death.

Another blooming loser is the carnation because of its association with official functions of unpleasant times past. Yes, for many, it's the Communist flower and is as popular as screw-top wine. Carnations are cheap and even a faux-pas, says one Pole. When asked what she thought about carnations, another Pole's evaluation was, "Eeeeeeeeeuh!" She explained that on Woman's Day in Communist times, women factory workers received carnations from their bosses.

You don't have to invest in an arrangement as big as a bush but remember the old rule that the bouquet should contain an odd number of blooms. But if it's more than nine, it doesn't matter—in that case, who would dare count and then complain? A single rose, by the way, should be presented bare without any frilly extras. If the flowers are wrapped in paper, you should rip it off before presenting them. Thrusting an unwieldy crinkly package into the hostess's face is gauche. Of course, that leaves you with a big wad of paper in your hand. I haven't figured that part out yet. It's okay to keep the clear plastic stuff on but leaving it on in a vase is like having plastic seat covers on your living room furniture.

Men, rather than women, should hand the flowers over to women (though male public figures do get giant bouquets shoved at them). Proper presentation is: First hold the flowers in your left hand, shake hands with host, and shift the flowers to your right hand for the presentation. For a surprise, carry them upside down behind your back, and then at the last moment with a flick of the wrist, flip them right-side-up and hear a gush of joy. Oh, and try not to hit the hapless recipient in the face. That takes the attention away from the flowers.

Christmas Spirit, Slavic Soul

The part of the Polish Christmas Eve dinner, *Wigilia*, that I like best is the breaking and sharing of the *opłatek*, the thin wafers that are on every table at Christmas eve. But this moment also reminds me how I lack Slavic Soul.

The chaos of getting a lot of people and heaps of food into the same room suddenly subsides at the *opłatek* moment. First, pieces of *opłatek* are distributed to each guest. Then, maneuvering around the long crowded table, you meet privately with every guest one by one: Huddled together and speaking in hushed voices, you exchange wishes for the next year. At the same time, you break off and eat a piece of each other's *opłatek*.

I like this tradition since you share a moment of intimacy with each person. The Christmas spirit pours into the room and billows at this very minute.

But here's the tricky part: If there are a lot of people at Wigilia, you have to be quick on your feet to think up various personal wishes. It's like having to come up with a series of Hallmark greeting card wishes in a row—except that they have to sound like something people really say. The Top Ten Hit List of Wigilia Wishes are: health, wealth, peace, love, success, happiness, longevity, fewer problems, pride in the children and simply, all the best. Poles have a knack for looking deep into your soul and putting into words what you really want. "I wish you success and satisfaction with your work, good colleagues and dear friends," I was told last year. "I wish you happiness in Poland even though you're far away from friends and family," said another.

Poles express their wishes so eloquently and sincerely that I get all choked up. By contrast, I feel cheap with my klutzy Polish, repeating stock wishes to different people. Determined to be as personal and heartfelt as I can, I look deeply in the person's eyes and say, "Uh, well... I wish you...um...ahem..." The person waits, blinks patiently, and then finally says, "Health and happiness?" I say, "Yes! Of course! Hah! That's it! I wish you health and happiness!" and move on to the next person: "Uh, well...I wish you...um..."

And then the kiddies. What should I say to them: "I wish you chocolate on a weekly basis," "I hope you don't get beat up at school anymore," or "I wish you fewer skinned knees for the next year"?

Perhaps the best wish someone could offer me for the coming year is that more of the Slavic Soul rubs off on me.

⑨ The Weirdest Christmas Ever

Around holiday time in Poland, I get anxious about my apparent lack of tradition. You can set your clock by the regularity and uniformity of Polish holidays and I worry that this social force will slowly blanket over my own cultural identity. When I ponder the highly ritualistic celebrations of my Polish in-laws, I naturally compare and question the worth of my own "traditions": Do I have any? Or am I just a sponge? Who am I? And why don't I own any Santa Claus candle holders?

I don't know the answers but I realize that when it comes to deep tradition, the scale will always be tipped in the Poles' favor.

One year at Christmas in the States, undaunted by the obvious imbalance, I bravely seized the opportunity to meld the holiday practices of my American family with those of my Polish husband's family. They were living in the States at the time and I decided to host both families in a cross-cultural Christmas. I envisioned a cultural hybrid of a holiday—a soft-focus warm fuzzy picture of us around a table: In spite of cultural differences, we would be laughing, talking, clinking our glasses and exchanging meaningful looks. You know, *sharing special moments*. The holiday meeting of two families from different cultures would be a wondrous and beautiful thing.

It was the weirdest Christmas ever.

From the start, the physical conditions were Polish only in that we would have far too many people in our small English-basement apartment in Washington, DC. And, nearly without discussion, it became clear that my mother-in-law would prepare the traditional twelve-dish *Wiglia* (Christmas Eve) dinner and the meat dishes for Christmas Day. I didn't object. Heck, my family would experience Polish *Wigilia* and besides, I never mind pawning off kitchen responsibilities of any kind. Several days in advance, my mother-in-law was off preparing The Big Dinner.

Now in my family, the big holiday tradition is sitting around drinking wine and arguing good naturedly about God-knows-what. At some point, we'll each visit the kitchen to do something, whether it be cooking, cleaning or just standing around talking to the people doing the actual work.

Of course, my mom and I decided to make the dish that we kids have demanded for years. You dump cream-of-mushroom soup on green beans and almonds, cover with that crispy canned onion stuff and heat. It ranks right up there with macaroni and cheese. Even though it's nothing exceptional, it's still the key to tradition: *Familiarity always tastes good.* Well, then, after that, we felt tired and had to sit down and relax with a glass of wine for conversation.

Meanwhile, for her Christmas Day *pasztet* (paté), my mother-in-law was off preparing the meat from a freshly-skinned rabbit she managed to buy somewhere out in the suburbs.

When the hour arrived for *Wigilia,* the group of us, 15 or so, sat down at the table. In my husband's household, this is a solemn moment—time to read from the Bible, say a prayer and share the *Wigilia* wafer (*opłatek*). In our household, it's time to pour the wine and listen to my father make a long, extemporaneous, ironic but tender toast while the food gets cold. Dueling traditions. What happened? The wafer made the rounds and each person broke off a piece. I was thrilled that my family would take part in this Polish tradition. As I turned to explain the ritual of sharing to my all-approving, super-tolerant, Protestant mother, she stuck her entire *opłatek* wafer piece in her mouth, munched a bit and told me, "Hmmmm, not bad."

Wait, it gets better.

At the end of the wafer ritual, my father stood, raised his wine glass and started his dinner speech. For my in-laws, alcohol is strictly off-limits at *Wigilia.* But, rising to the occasion, they took a few symbolic sips. My husband and his sister oohed and ahhed over all the traditional Polish dishes of pierogi, herring, and poppy seed. And that dumb bean casserole sure tasted like Christmas to me too.

Then my family got to our part of the tradition. For the last 15 years, our friends in Wales (another story) have sent us Christmas Crackers. These are party-favor-like-things which you yank apart. They explode with a crack! and a little prize, a joke and a tissue-paper crown drop out. So as we've done for years, my family put on our silly party hats, read off the jokes, compared prizes and continued to drink our wine. It's a ludicrous practice compared to the weight of the Polish Catholic tradition of prayer, emotion and worship. But, hey, like the green beans, it's ours.

It wasn't very Polish, sitting around the *Wigilia* table wearing silly party hats. Blessings on my parents-in-law: They hesitated, studied this strange scene but eventually donned their goofy hats too. Recently, I asked my mother-in-law how she remembered that dinner and those hats. "It was a nice surprise. It was like celebrating New Year," she said, "And we looked great in the pictures." I asked my mother what she remembered and she asked, "Isn't that when you cooked the turkey upside down?" No, Mom, that was Thanksgiving. Then she recalled, "Oh, yes! All those mushroom pierogis!" and we reminisced about the fabulous spread my mother-in-law had prepared.

I'm not sure if that cross-cultural Christmas experience will ever be repeated and I know we didn't meld any traditions. But there was warmth in its oddity. Each family got something familiar. And each family understood what brought comfort to the other. So maybe it wasn't what I had expected but it did turn out to be a cross-cultural hybrid of a celebration—everyone found comfort both in strangeness and familiarity at the same time. In my case, I guess that the powerful force behind Polish traditions is becoming my cultural identity. It's becoming more familiar and therefore comforting. But I won't let go completely. If I ever host a Christmas for my in-laws, I'll have to get party hats and make that dumb green-bean casserole.

Other Curiosities

⑨ One Hell of a Romantic Trip

"Adventurers who fall in love with someone from another culture end up with much more than an exotic holiday. If you succeed, you're on that trip for a lifetime," Diane Dicks writes of intercultural romances, in Cupid's Wild Arrows. Combine her analysis with the conventional wisdom that marriage is hell and you're on a lifetime journey to hell.

Like all journeys, the bicultural one is engrossing but perhaps more complex than the monocultural one. My husband is Polish and many of my North American friends are married to or involved with Poles. I think we'd all agree that *complex* is a key concept here.

A bicultural couple has problems similar to other couples' but the twist to their marital burdens demands extra tolerance. Monocultural couples might argue about family: "Does your mother have to stay two weeks with us? Why not with your sister?" A Polish-American couple might have a different focus: "Does your mother have to live with us? Why not with your sister?"

And indeed, family is an extra complex issue. North Americans in Poland have to adjust to a higher rate of family intervention in the couple's everyday life. As the Polish saying goes, *Nie żenisz się z kobietą, ale z jej rodziną* (You don't marry a woman, you marry a family—which goes for the guy too). An American married to Pole says, "You renovate an apartment, your father-in-law is helping you and it becomes a family matter." That can be a joy or a burden. If the North American resists the family tendrils, the Polish partner might have to step in or explain ("Mom, leave him alone").

Then there's the language thing. It's already tough enough to express deep thoughts and feelings in your native tongue ("If I find your dirty underwear on the floor again, I'll kill you"). And cross-cultural couples do confess to language problems. Says a Canadian married to a Pole: "She doesn't understand big words in English and I don't understand even small ones in Polish." An American dating a Pole says, "Whenever we're on a serious subject, I'm groping for words." Plus, he says, speaking in Polish all the time can be tiring.

A wider issue is humor and cultural references. This takes the fun out of saying a guy in the street looks like Mr. Rogers, says an American. By the time he describes how dweeby Mr. Rogers is, the hilarity is lost. So the risk is that your foreign partner may never know exactly how uproariously funny and witty you are.

The social life of intercultural couples varies. For some, it's not easy to find people in whose company both partners feel totally comfortable and appreciated. If one partner isn't fluent in the other language, the two might lead independent social lives. Or they make sacrifices, hanging out with people they don't understand. One partner might dominate socially. For example, my Polish is good enough to participate in conversations but it's not good enough to be as loud and obnoxious as I am in English. So my husband dominates our Polish social life and our Polish friends think I'm a polite demure American. Our English-speaking friends know the truth.

When it comes to the domestic drudgery scene, North American men and Polish women probably work out the best deal. Polish women are more apt to accept the bulk of household duties and most North American guys will pitch in. A Polish woman says of her Canadian husband, "He can live on his own. Sometimes he makes dinner, sometimes I do. I wanted it this way but didn't think it was possible." What a dreamboat! American women wouldn't get that help from the traditional Polish he-man. But that type is a dying breed anyway, says a Pole who gladly shares household chores with his American partner.

When you get down to the meat of it, an intercultural relationship is like any other: It's based on mutual compatibility and give-and-take. But when two people come from different value systems, it just takes more of everything: open-mindedness, tolerance, sacrifice and effort. Writer Diane Dicks wonders about cross-cultural relationships, "Don't they have some advantages? Doesn't the extra tolerance they demand help form a better relationship?" I think the answer is yes. And once you find that special hell you both can live with, it's definitely an interesting trip getting there. And well worth the price of the ticket.

⑨ Lip Action

Everybody knows the ol' Polish One Two Three; when Polish friends greet each other, they exchange three kisses on the cheeks. Usually, the first kiss gets placed on recipient's right cheek to avoid a collision of schnozzes. If both parties wear glasses, there's less cheek-to-cheek contact and something more like air-kissing; otherwise the kissers emerge from the greeting with spectacles askew. Sometimes for a more casual greeting friends will bestow one kiss only. One development in Polish lip and cheek action is planting all three smooches on one cheek—an economy of affection between friends. Kissing routines, by the way, are for man/woman or woman/woman encounters between people who know each other fairly well. Men usually just shake hands unless they're good friends who haven't seen each other for a while; bear hugs and maybe kisses, then, are in order.

There is a peck of another color and that is, of course, hand-kissing—a tradition rarely practiced by "modern" Poles. Older Polish men often kiss women's hands in social situations, especially formal ones, but rarely in professional ones. An older woman gets her hand kissed more often than a young one, but in any case, laying a gentle smooch on a woman's hand is considered a sign of old-fashioned respect.

Women's reactions to hand-kissing varies. Some Polish women like the tradition, and others are so used to it they don't care one way or another. Some younger Polish women say they don't like having their hands nuzzled, but their attitudes might change with time since the ritual is adopted with age—if it doesn't die out with younger generations.

Some American women just accept hand pecks at cultural face-value, and others consider it sexist and prefer to exchange firm grips. A few unaccustomed to the gesture melt, hearts a-flutter, and their eyes roll back.

Men: If you aspire to hand-kissing, the easiest way is to take the woman's right hand and cradle it almost flat in your right hand (or both of your hands if you wish to beef up the charm factor). Bend at the waist and bow your head to her hand. Lifting her hand high up to your lips is a no-no. If you happen to be considerably taller than she, you will yank her arm out of the socket. The kiss doesn't get laid on the fingers but on the back of the hand. A big wet one is not the desired effect so lips should brush the hand lightly. Whatever you do, don't make a loud smacking noise or use your tongue. Avoid slobbering at all costs.

Women: Older Poles might kiss your hand but some don't. I've often made the mistake of gripping a gentleman's hand with the intention of giving a firm shake and end up with a clumsy twist in mid-air as he wrestles a kiss onto the back of my hand. A distinguished Polish woman well seasoned in receiving official hand-smacks says she always extends her hand rather listlessly avoid this hand-grappling. This ambiguous gesture is much better than sticking your arm straight out with a limp wrist in anticipation of adoration. If you insist on avoiding the whole affair, grab the fellow's hand with an iron-clad grip and pump it heartily several times. However, be aware that you risk surprising him, offending him, or breaking his nose as he bows to ritual.

It does happen that a man and a woman will shake hands and then he'll kiss her hand too. Nothing wrong with compromise.

◎ Manners 101

At a flea market in the States, I bought a funny old typewriter that was very heavy. The man who sold it to me watched me struggle awhile with the unwieldy thing before offering his help. I accepted. "I didn't know if I should ask or not," he said, "You never know these days." Well, a Polish man knows. He has to carry the damn thing.

Oh, those Polish gentlemanly civilities; they make up the well-understood code of manners for men in Poland. This code doesn't match the "modern" American notion of behavior for the sexes—egalitarian and non-sexist. But "modern" doesn't guarantee a passing grade in Manners 101 in Poland. There are some clashes here so make your own choices on how you want to act—and react—in a different culture.

Walking—easy enough. But in Poland, a man should not walk in front of a woman companion. If he does, he might as well stick his finger up his nose too. Unless, of course, only he knows the way—say, through a maze of offices. Then he should explain that he'll show her the way. Once my Polish husband walked in front of me into a building and his friend scolded him for leaving his good manners back in the States. I hadn't noticed.

And then there's the door issue. A man opens doors for women. Period. He might even wait to hold the door for an approaching woman. She should say *dziękuję* or at least acknowledge it with a friendly nod (but many don't). An American woman said that in the States she's not surprised when unknown men let doors shut in front of her. But she also finds it rude after living in Poland. An American man says it doesn't matter who holds the door: "Polite people open doors and polite people say thank you." He says that sometimes women hold doors for him in the States. Polish men would find that embarrassing.

In Poland, a man should *always* carry heavy things for a woman and will get strange looks if he doesn't. American women might appreciate the help but they wouldn't expect an automatic offer. One American woman even reads it this way: "It's like saying you're incapable if he automatically jumps in and helps you." Wow. She says my flea market man was right to hesitate. By contrast, the Polish view seems to be, well, men are stronger so they *should* carry things. A real Polish gentleman will even carry a manageable bag for woman, her purse excepted of course.

Helping a woman on with a coat isn't as strict a rule but it's a sign of good manners. No man ever helped me on with my coat during my last trip to the States. Okay, so it was August, but it doesn't happen regularly even in winter.

What about paying? The general convention is that the man pays for outings—or at least pretends to. "I can't imagine it any other way," says a 32 year-old Polish woman who passes her wallet to her husband who rarely carries cash. But on the dating scene, this rule doesn't always hold; young lovebirds will often share expenses willingly, especially after the first date.

A Polish man who doesn't extend the basic gentlemanly courtesies is thought *prymityw* (primitive), *źle wychowany* (badly brought up) or *cham* (a clod or a boor). Foreign men who don't are, well, foreign.

⑨ Expat Culture

You're a North American in Poland. One day you wake up and realize you're part of a new culture. It's not the way you'd behave at home, yet it's not quite Polish either. Welcome to Expat Culture. At first, you feel a little sheepish about some things but eventually you succumb and become a full-blown member.

Here are a few characteristics of our local Expat Culture:

1. Expats like going to McDonald's or other fast food joints and don't feel embarrassed about it. It tastes great. Expats deep into The Culture even admit this in public *without shame*.

2. Even though they're not usually joiners, people find themselves participating in organizations like Foot Lovers Discussion Group, The Welsh Yodlers Curry Dance Club, or The Tuesday Night Math Club.

3. Expats carry around ugly plastic bags, some printed with beach scenes or pictures of cuddly kittens with bows on their heads. After a while, they don't even notice—or care—what's on the bag.

4. Social horizons expand and stretch like putty. People meet, socialize and make friends with folks with whom they'd never have contact back home. Sometimes this means types you'd normally avoid. Or really interesting people who wouldn't give you the time of day at home. Sometimes they're just freaks but you like them.

5. Expats make grammar mistakes, blank out on simple vocabulary words or construct strange sentences like, "Call to me in the moment you leave" or "I've never met that word."

6. For some reason, some American expats adopt British question intonation and vocabulary like "flat" for the American "apartment." Maybe they think British elements sound more continental or sophisticated. Brits might interpret this as a linguistic surrender.

7. Expats have forgotten what it's like to live with an ice-maker, clothes dryer and garbage disposal in the sink. They wonder if such things are really necessary.

8. Singles are thrilled to find themselves dating types of people who wouldn't look sideways at them back home.

⑨ Reality Check

Wow! How nice! Great! That's fantastic! I had a terrific time! It was wonderful! Have a nice day!

Americans. So damn cheerful.

To some extent, Poles enjoy the upbeat American pom-pom shaking cheer. Who would dare claim that cheerfulness is bad? But sometimes Poles balk at American-style frothy enthusiasm. Ask a Pole to imitate American behavior and chances are the result will include a wide smile, an elongated "Woooow!" and "Everything is fine!" with a thumbs-up.

One Pole said, "My first impression was how happy Americans must be." But like many Poles she cracked the code: "Poles have different expectations. Something "fantastic" for Americans would not be "fantastic" to my way of thinking." Another Pole says, "When Americans say it was great, I know it was good. When they say it was good, I know it was okay. When they say it was okay, I know it was bad."

All this Yankee mega-cheery stuff isn't a crime; it's just confusing. When Poles hear again and again how wonderful! great! and fine! things are, they don't know what to believe or how to react. Or where they stand, complains a Pole. During training, when giving participants on-the-spot evaluations, we list all the good points before getting to the meaty criticism. Sometimes people interrupt and say, "Yes, yes, I know. Great. Great. Great. How did I really do?"

Poles expect people to be direct with emotions, views and reactions. A Pole who lived in the States and works with Americans says, "I'm the kind of person whose face reflects my feelings. When someone is feeling down but poses as happy, I don't like it. Sometimes it gets on my nerves." Poles, it seems, are in a constant state of reality check.

I believe that Americans sometimes feel pressured to be upbeat, can-do and gung-ho. Too much of that irritates me and other long-term American expats in Poland: "If you want smarmy American optimism, call someone else," an old American pal recently told me. In any case, I think I know where it comes from. The underlying belief is you create your own happiness—a carryover of the Protestant work ethic—so you want to relay success, confidence or at least competence. Plus, Americans don't want to burden others or put a damper on things with negativity. One American says that Americans "cover up their nervousness and fear of mistakes by being really friendly."

Polish culture places a high value on honest expression of your emotions. Plus you behave seriously to establish your credibility as honest, fair and reliable. Poles respect modesty, so you just don't find as many great-wow-fantastic exchanges in everyday Polish conversation. Their expressions of joy, approval or support are simply more low-key. Americans interpret that as reserved, unenthusiastic or not confident.

"Americans are too cheerful and Poles are too depressing," a Pole concludes. So is there hope for communication? Yes. I think that Americans find relief when there's no social stigma for deviating from the put-on-a-happy-face approach. And Poles are increasingly attracted to the everyday results of positive thinking and feel-good optimism. In fact, I suspect that Polish scientists are hunched over petri dishes in a lab, culturing their own strain of optimism—responding to the new reality check in Poland these days.

⑨ Bureaucracy Fun and Games

Documents, stamps and notaries. Long waits, grumpy clerks, and frustration. Poland has bureaucracy down to an art form; Franz Kafka must be cuddling up in his grave.

Here's the typical hair-tearing scene in a Polish bureaucratic office: you go in, say, to register a car. The clerk tells you which documents to bring in. Later you return with the papers and the clerk says, "Your father's name is Brad so you need a special permit for your dog to ride with his nose out the window." You fly into a rage, "But I don't have a dog!" The answer, of course, is, "But you might get one. Those are the rules." So you return later with the document, register your car and leave the office feeling bitter relief.

And that's when things are going well. When you venture into the dark mysterious depths of Polish bureaucracy, it's a black hole. A Pole applied to the Administration of Apartments in Mokotów to acquire unowned attic space in a building. He spent two years fulfilling the so-called requirements, but there was always something missing. In total, he provided 40 documents and lost $5,000 in application fees. In the end, the head of the office called him and said, "We're getting rid of you." Later he learned a more "connected" person got the space. Something else stinks there but the point is that no one had to provide him with an explanation. There is no great obligation for Polish bureaucrats to provide clear information or be accountable. But he is suing the office.

Sometimes Polish bureaucrats can't provide information or decent service even if they want to—laws and regulations change often and the public reads about it in the press. But because desk officers haven't received official information or guidelines, they don't know how to do their jobs or even field inquiries. In one case, the chain of command for building permit approvals changed; while the new law was already in effect, it stymied the permit office. They admitted they didn't know *how* to get applications approved. "I knew more than they did," says a Polish builder whose business depends on the approval process. The office eventually sorted itself out but the wait cost him time and money.

One horror story involves a Canadian entrepreneur and his Serbian wife who need visas in order to obtain work permits for employment in their own catering company. Like the Pole and the attic space, he has expended disproportionate time and energy on bureaucracy: "In the last 15 months, we have spent over a solid 30+ days in various government offices." In the end, they decided to leave Poland. When they cancelled the application and requested a refund for the work permit application fee (1,200 złotys), an office clerk called three times to inform them that one change on the application would push it through.

Earlier, the visa office had promised them temporary residence so it looked encouraging...until they were told their temporary residence applications were insufficient: They would have apply all over again. This included redoing taxes from 5 years ago to generate one missing tax record (they did so and the case officer expressed surprise). So the entrepreneur and his wife will give the application process one last shot. If it doesn't work, he will turn down a contract from a large food corporation to help grow their business, and dividends from his Polish investments will go to Serbia, their current home. "I just want to be told if my wife, my investments and I are not welcome in Poland. Stop dicking us around," he says.

This case (among others) prompted the American Chamber of Commerce in Poland to set up the Visa Committee, which lobbies for changes in regulations for residency and works permits; they're pushing to merge the dual live-and-work procedures like other countries do. And as in other countries, Polish legislation is designed to protect domestic employment but the problem is that it doesn't necessarily differentiate between an underwear peddler and someone with expertise and potential to grow the economy.

"One of the problems is the quality of civil servants—they're underpaid and young without business or life experience," says Dorota Dąbrowska, Executive Director of the Chamber, "They don't have judgement and are tied to procedure. We can't change them or their salaries but we can improve legislation and the procedures." And by the way, she notes, members of EU countries might have to go through the same application process to work in Poland.

Maybe Polish bureaucracy isn't much worse than in other European countries but it demoralizes Poles and foreigners alike—something Poland can't afford to do.

⑨ Ethno-types in Stereo

After visiting the States, Poles often remark on the cushy material life: comfy cars, homes and conveniences. Attempting to bust the myth of living on Easy Street, an American explains: "We work really hard for those things." It sounds reasonable, but Poles might digest the message as "We Americans work hard, you Poles don't." Yikes! The well-intentioned myth-buster becomes a stereotype: the superior American. Some Yanks just need to tone it down.

The type of American who wants to "help change things in Poland" or "teach Poles" may not get the round of applause they expect. In fact, Poles might perceive them as patronizing do-gooders. A Pole complains about ten-hour work days and an American says, "Oh, that's normal in the States." The Pole feels put down, like a whiny weakling. Some American visitors discuss principles of democracy with a group of prominent and highly educated Poles; the Poles come away complaining they've been talked down to, like children.

Not the picture of blissful cultural exchanges.

The stereotype of Americans includes over-confidence, know-it-allism and lack of awareness of "different ways." And these negative perceptions of the Yank are compounded by the fact that pointing out differences is sometimes interpreted as criticism.

Negative impressions of Americans have to do with ethnocentrism. Americans are often perceived as shoving their values and norms of behavior down others' throats. Their assumption, it appears, is that others want to be like Americans. After all, the USA is a world power and the standard of living is high. Heck, why wouldn't people want to be like Americans and want their advice? Again, that sounds reasonable (cough)—except it's ethnocentric.

So what are Americans supposed to do? Tiptoe around those who might believe that Yanks are imposing their values by giving assistance or information? That Americans are dumping on Poland by commenting on differences? Or criticizing by making suggestions?

Here's another toughie: Americans are welcomed to Poland and in many cases, invited. They arrive and get the idea that Poles suffer from an inferiority complex and resent the American view on how things should be. Americans might get frustrated by what they see as over-sensitivity on the part of Poles. And, yes, Poles might get defensive—that's what happens when you feel underappreciated. Poland is less developed than the States but Poles don't see that as a reason to relinquish time-honored values and pride, buying in to an identity that comes from the outside.

Many Poles and Americans feel these undercurrents of tension, and no divining rod points to a specific source. But consider this: A Pole says that some Americans, after a couple of years here, learn to adjust their approach to "teaching": They tone down their roles as educators and do some of their own learning from Poles. As a result, Poles appreciate their contributions. That's a successful cultural exchange. I think what this means is that Poles want—and appreciate—know-how, advice and assistance from abroad. But they want it from people who understand and appreciate Poland. There are plenty of Americans—and Westerners in general—who simply like Poland and Poles and want to exchange experiences. It just takes time and effort to find an exchange rate that both sides can live with.

A Language Booster

⑨ Six and Violins

Some numbers are more famous than others. Number One, for example, means success and glory. Shouting out, "We're Number Six!" just doesn't cut it. A four-letter word gets attention while a five-letter one goes unnoticed. Everybody knows it's three cheers and not two or four.

I don't like numbers much. I prefer adjectives. But I'll admit begrudgingly that numbers enjoy higher status in the world than adjectives do. Unfortunately, I have a hard time with numbers in Polish—and I'm not alone. Numbers have confounded far better Polish language learners than me.

In fact, numbers in a foreign language are often tricky especially when the counting system is different. For example, in English, 199 is "one hundred *and* ninety-nine," but in French it's "one hundred, four-twenty, nineteen." And in Yoruba, an African language, it's "two hundred less one." A linguist from Michigan State University, Dennis Preston, pointed out to me that no matter how fluent second-language speakers are, they almost always count in their mother tongue. This indicates to me that numbers in our native language are linguistic brain barnacles.

One thing that frustrates me is that Polish numbers all sound alike to me—all those *tysiąc*'s (thousands) and *dziesiąt*'s (tens). (Of course, a Pole could say the same about English: 13 sounds like 30, 15 like 50.) I get Numeral Anxiety attacks. As soon a discussion about costs, dates or statistics comes up, my brain puts up the barricades and hauls up the drawbridge—numerical enemies approaching!

Let me state my case more clearly. In Polish, the number one is treated like an adjective. The numbers two, three and four differ grammatically from numbers five and above. The number two is either *dwa, dwaj, dwie* or *dwoje* and, when declined, totals 13 different forms—more than any other numeral. My favorite part of all this is a "special category" of nouns (insanity-causing exceptions)—violins, doors, scissors, children—that require their very own number form. With some number forms, you have to change the verb form also. I don't want to be accused of doing tabloid grammar here but this stuff can give you nightmares.

After listening to me describe this incredible system, a Spanish friend said, "Now I understand why Ludwig Zamenhof invented Esperanto." Zamenhof, a Pole, designed the language for international use. And wouldn't you know it, one of his Esperanto grammar rules says numbers don't change grammatical form. So he even recognized the brain-busting potential of numbers in Polish.

But let's not think that way.

One night, I heard a man speak who advised us not to think of things as "difficult." For example, instead of thinking of Polish as "difficult," he viewed all the irregularities of the language as its "charm." That encouraged me. I never realized that when it comes to numbers, I could be so charming.

⑨ A Rootin' Tootin' Good Time

Every once in a while, it's important to bear down and bone up on colorful language. No, that doesn't mean dirty words but "reduplication"—when the sounds of a word are repeated. Reduplication is typical of children's language like *choo-choo, eensy-weensy* and *nighty-night*. A great amount of onomatopoeia also depends on reduplication: *pitter-patter, bow-wow, ding-dong.*

But reduplication isn't limited to sounds, kiddie words and cutesy-wutesy talk. There are grown-up reduplication words too. For example, "hanky-panky" is certainly an adult concept. And many reduplications are just busting with linguistic appeal.

Example: Fuddy-duddies are humdrum company and wishy-washy folks make so-so big wigs. Joe Blow from the go-go bar would get a no-go from hoity-toity types. Lovey-dovey couples make goo-goo eyes at each other. We avoid riff-raff and wheeler-dealers in higgledy-piggledy, helter-skelter, pell-mell situations. And when we want to pooh-pooh something, we create spontaneous reduplications by adding the Yiddish consonant cluster *schm-:* "Hurry, we'll be late!" "Awww, late, schmate, who cares?"

Folks, we're doin' the linguistic boogie-woogie here.

Some other languages do the hokey-pokey even more than English. For example, reduplication carries more linguistic weight in Austronesian languages, spoken anywhere there's good weather: Hawaii, Easter Island, Madagascar and Polynesia, to name a few spots. In the language of the Philippines, Tagalog, the future tense is a reduplicative form: *Takbuh* means "run," *tatakbuh* means "will run." In Somali, it gives a meaning of space: *Fen* means "gnaw at," *fen-fen* means "gnaw at on all sides." In Indonesian, there's a plural sense: *Anak* is "child" and *anak anak* means "all sorts of children." In some creole languages, reduplication can intensify meaning: In English-based Creoles, *talktalk* means to chatter and *looklook* means to stare. Remember all of this on your next trip to Bora Bora.

Another super-duper thing about reduplication: It makes words easy to remember. Here are some examples in Polish that you can whip out to impress your friends (for some reason, many of the examples I found refer to low-quality conversation):

Gadki-szmatki is something like "talking rags" from *gadać* (to blab). *My tu gadu-gadu* means "We're blabbing here." If someone is using empty talk, you can say *trele-morele,* which is like a sarcastic "Yeah, yeah, sure right." If you want to be direct with someone who's feeding you B.S., you say, *"Sraty taty."* When someone is saying stupid things or trying to cheat you, it's *koszałki-opałki.*

Ever squabble with someone and then realize you're both arguing the same point? You put a stop this *smoje boje*—battling for the same thing.

Something which is so-so is *jako-tako.*

Robić bara-bara is hanky-panky and, like its English equivalent, the word is humorous, not vulgar. *Fiku-miku* has similar associations even though it comes from a children's rhyme.

In Polish there's *hocus-pocus* which is the same as *czary-mary*. And Poles have started saying *bye-bye*. If someone makes a joke that you find distinctly unfunny, say with a straight face, *Śmichu-chichu* (Ha-ha).

So there you have it: Reduplication is not just goody-goody talk for weenies. In some languages, it's meaty linguistic stuff and in others it's spice. Of course, there are reduplications in a different category altogether: Holy Moley, rodger-dodger, yabba-dabba-doo, scoobie-doobie-doo. We'll just file those under "Hodgepodge."

⑨ The Ritual of Liquid Charm

One night at a get-together, my Polish host asked me to make a toast in English. "Um, cheers," I offered lamely. He shot me a look of pity and graciously pointed out that I was a native speaker of a language linguistically deficient in toasts. And it's true. I am hard-pressed to think of more than a few toasts in English: There's "To your health," and "Cheers," the less elegant "Bottoms up," and the corny "To us." These are remarkably dull and unoriginal compared to the Polish possibilities. Languages typically reflect social realities and this is certainly true of Polish and the ritual of sharing a drink. The language is rich in toasts and there's one for every situation.

Many Americans report that they don't normally drink shots of hard alcohol at home but enjoy doing so in Poland. This has to do with the atmosphere of warmth and camaraderie created by the ritualistic consumption of alcohol. Okay, okay, so slovenly consumption can create warm fuzzies too, but we're looking at tradition here. The basic rules of imbibing are simple: Alcohol is poured around the table into miniature glasses, you lift your glass as someone makes a toast, and as a group you knock it back. Chances are this will happen again (and again and again) during evenings of special celebrations. The all-purpose toasts (that means "safe") in Polish are *Sto lat* (may you live one hundred years) and *Na zdrowie* (to your health). It's also common to make toasts to the meeting, *Za spotkanie* (to our meeting/gathering) or to people, *Zdrowie gospodarzy* (to the health of the host).

Then things get a little more colorful (less refined). A common one is *Rybka lubi pływać* (The little fish likes to swim—from the vodka and herring tradition). There's *Po całym* (Bottoms up) and *Jan Sebastian Bach* (*bach,* a pun for "take a slug"). The unofficial presidential toast, popularized by Wałęsa, goes *Zdrowie wasze, w gardła nasze* (To your health, in our throats).

There's also a wide collection of hard-core toasts not recommended for polite company. To name just a few: *Chluśniem bo uśniem* (Let's drink lest we fall asleep). *No to chlup, w ten głupi dziub* (A splash into this stupid beak) and *Pierdykniem bo odwykniem* (Let's knock it back so we don't dry out). The English translations just don't do these ditties justice.

The toasting system is so elaborate that there are even toasts for different times in the evening. The first toast of the evening could be *Odpalamy silniki* (Let's start the motors). Later in the evening, you might drink *Na drugą nóżkę* (For the second leg). A call for *Karniaka* (a penalty) helps a late-comer catch up on the drinking. *No to strzemiennego* (for the stirrups) is similar to the suggestion in English to have a drink "for the road" (NOT a good idea in a country where the police take your first-born child for driving under the influence).

Sometimes, when something significant is said, no toast is made but the drinkers may empty their glasses in unison to signal agreement or respect. There's even an anti-toast to signal that you are specifically NOT drinking to the topic at hand. For example, a friend described her nightmarish tax problems to me. "Here's not to taxes," I said, lilting my glass. *Na pochybel,* she substituted, an expression in Old Polish from for "a killing" which means roughly "Down with that."

The list of toasts is long: There are military themes, puns, rhymes, sexist, cynical, bawdy and downright vulgar ones. Actually, you can cook up a toast to anything or anyone—and in any way you like. It's the warmth, wit and symbolism that count in lifting the glass together. Like telling jokes, the important thing is to know your audience. It's not a good idea to announce *Pijem aż oślepniem, palim aż ogłuchniem* (Let's drink 'til we go blind, let's smoke 'til we go deaf) if Grandma is sitting at the table.

ⓖ Thanksaroonie

Thank you. Thank you very much. Thanks a lot. Thanks a million. Thanks a bunch. Much obliged.

You can't say it too many times. But of course you've got to know how to say it. In Polish, thank you is *dziękuję* and the most common response is *proszę* or *proszę bardzo*.

Dzięki is a jaunty informal thanks and if you want to speak for several bodies, say *dziękujemy* (we thank you). Express a smidgen more gratitude with *dziękuję bardzo* (thank you very much) but reverse the order to *bardzo dziękuję* for more oompf. Smoosh in extra appreciation with *dziękujemy pięknie* or *ślicznie* (We thank you beautifully). *Dziękuję serdecznie* (heartfeltedly) administers a larger dose of serious thanks for bigger favors. You wouldn't say it when someone passes you the salt, for example.

Occasionally you'll hear Poles say *dziękuję* when they get off the elevator, as if they're thanking you for sharing the space with them.

This is exceedingly proper behavior. Sometimes parents will announce *dziękuję* to their children and that means scram, leave the room or go to bed. *Dziękuję z góry* (thanks from above) means thanks in advance.

In some cultures (like Japan and India) gratitude is expressed by acknowledging indebtedness in terms like "I'm so indebted to you that, in humiliation, I must jump off a cliff immediately." In Polish the gratitude game is played a little differently.

A Polish neighbor fixed an American's refrigerator for her so she slathered on the thanks. He denied that he had done anything exceptional; *of course* he would help her, he was her neighbor after all. "I felt like I was thanking too *much,*" the American said. But she was right to thank away; that's the way the game is played. Undying flowery gratitude is extended and, in response, the favor is downplayed with heaps of modesty.

A computer techie did me a mammoth time-consuming favor. I bought him a big bottle of champagne and told him he was my hero. He responded according to the rules: Claiming it was nothing, he looked like he wanted to crawl under the table and die quickly and quietly from embarrassment.

To play down the fact that you've actually done something decent, in Polish you say, *Nie ma za co* or *Nie ma sprawy* which is like "It was nothing."

Americans sometimes will deny the worth of their actions too ("Don't mention it" or "It was nothing"), but less dramatically. After all, if we act like huge favors are just trifles, the person might ask for even bigger favors. Horrors! Besides, when somebody thanks us for doing something extra nice (and maybe troublesome), there's nothing wrong with basking in a little appreciation and gratitude.

So there might be a little more emotional maneuvering in a heartfelt thank-you between Poles: more words, more locked eye contact and a firmer handshake. And thanks in general should be delivered as personally as possible. This means the thank-you card is *out* in Poland. Sending thanks on paper to relatives and friends seems stilted or just plain strange to Poles. A proper Polish thank-you for a gift is one or three kisses on the cheeks. So if a Polish friend gives you a present, pucker up. It's much better than jumping off a cliff.

◎ The Tune of Bye

If good-byes were music, Americans would whistle a simple tune and Poles would play a five-part harmony.

As in English, there are plenty of ways to say goodbye but the musical score of parting ways in Polish is more elaborate. *Do widzenia* is your generic good-bye and *do zobaczenia* means see you later. *Cześć* is the informal bye. Kids say *pa-pa* (bye-bye) but adults use just *pa* for a cutesy, friendly effect. *Na razie* and its very slangy variant *na ra* are roughly the equivalent of "so long," and *do następnego razu* is "until next time." The younger set says *hej*, a jaunty version of bye like *ciao*. And *żegnaj* means farewell. If you're stuffing someone into a train, plane or car, say *miłej podróży (bon voyage* or have a nice trip) or *szerokiej drogi* (literally, "wide road" meaning have a safe trip). Some folks will say *z bogiem* (May God be with you).

But that's only part of the Polish good-bye song. Memorizing and blurting out the correct phrase doesn't mean you're singing the right song for parting ways with Poles. Foreigners who say bye and zip out the door strike Poles as curt, cold or just plain ill-mannered. Poles might even feel emotionally gypped since some situations call for a more elaborate ritual. "Poles do everything with flourish," an American says, "They can't just say 'see ya.'"

Indeed, Poles tend to linger more over good-byes; it's part of the tradition of not letting visitors go and prolonging the visit. You thank and compliment each other, talk about the success of the evening and the next get-together. Even though *wszystkiego najlepszego* (best wishes) is the standard phrase for special occasions, toss it in for bonus politeness points. *Powodzenia* (all the best) adds extra floweriness as well. Of course, you have to get all those cheek kisses in there too. Americans, by contrast, might practice a briefer method of affectionate slugs, hugs and see-ya-laters. Or maybe just a jaunty wave good-bye.

During good-bye conversations, it's gracious to send regards to family members by saying *pozdrów Marka* (regards to Marek), or the more cuddly *ucałowania dla Marka* (kisses for Marek). Add *trzymaj się* which means something like "Hang in there": a nice thing to add especially when a friend is having hard time. On the phone even an everyday good-bye between friends includes verbal smooches like *całuję Cię* (I kiss you), *buźka* (a kiss) or *buziaczki* (a cute form of kisses).

For Poles, it's just plain politeness to see someone to the door whether you're at home or the office. At least stand up to say goodbye—unless you have a really good excuse, like a broken leg. Waving and saying bye to a small group of people is okay but shaking everyone's hand is more polite, especially in formal situations. Since you're supposed to do the same upon arriving, your total contact with some people might amount to this: "*Dobry wieczór*" (good evening) and then, three hours later, "*Do widzenia*" (goodbye). I always feel a little sheepish about this since it highlights the zero contact I had with some folks. I would prefer a slip-out-the-back-jack maneuver but this is rude.

When seeing someone off at the train station or airport, Poles will often wave until the person is out of sight—it's as poetic as it is polite. So when you really like people, change your tune and do the same. In fact, accompany people right to the street. Then chase their car down the block—yip and howl with sadness for a memorable effect.

So remember, if your good-bye tune is too short and simple, the effect in Poland might be, "Here's your hat. There's the door. What's your hurry?" Or, as one of my buddies likes to say, "Seeya-loveya-meanit-bye." In other words, if your good-bye is too short, it comes across as a sorry song.

⑨ Pan, Pani, or Hey You?

Pani? Pani Beata? Beata? Deciding between the first name and the formal Pan (Sir) or Pani (Madam) in Polish can cause some discomfort for English speakers not used to distinguishing between familiar and polite terms of address.

Many languages use what linguists call the T and V address system (after the French use of the second-person personal pronouns [you]: *tu* is informal and *vous* is formal). Like French, the Polish informal address is the second-person singular form as in *ty jesteś* (you are), usually dropping the *ty* pronoun altogether. The formal address, Pan or Pani, calls for the third-person singular form of the verb: *Pan jest...* (Sir is...).

The choice of address term indicates the relationship. Young people usually call each other by their first names right away. Otherwise, you address an unfamiliar face as Pani or if you know the last name, *Pani Fiłonowicz*. As you get to know her a little better, you might call her *Pani Beata* and someday, just *Beata*. The big question for many foreigners is when and how to advance to this informal stage.

There is an old ritual of moving to the first-name *ty* basis called a *Bruderszaft* (German for "brotherhood") in which Pan or Pani announces to you, *Wypijmy Bruderszaft* (Let's drink a *Bruderszaft*). You entwine your arms with a shot of vodka in hand, drink, and reintroduce yourselves with first names. An American who learned about this custom was disappointed when a Polish colleague nonchalantly suggested they use the *ty* form. The American inquired about a *Bruderszaft*. "Well, okay," the Pole said, "We can do it," as if it were whimsy, and they went out for a beer. So much for old rituals.

Addressing a stranger with *ty* indicates that something is wrong with the relationship; it's as jolting as saying to an American, "Hey, you!" In the event of a car accident, the other driver might bolt from his car screaming, *Głupi jesteś*?! (Are you stupid?!). A Polish actor, graduated from the National Drama School in Warsaw, speaks better Polish than the average Pole. Born to a Polish mother and a black African father, he doesn't look very Polish with his light brown skin and head of dreadlocks. He says he's sometimes addressed by strangers in the *ty* form. "It's an expression of racism," he says.

Using *Pan* or *Pani* and the third-person singular verb is sign of respect, and the honorific goes a step farther by including the person's title, such as *Pani Profesor* or *Pan Dyrektor* (though sometimes good friends will call address each other as *pan* or *pani* for irony). In very rare cases, some parents enjoy this grammatical honor. I heard my Polish husband say to his mother, *Czy Mama chce herbaty?* (Does Mama want tea?). My first reaction was to say, "I don't know, why don't you ask her?" wondering how he could talk about his mother as if she weren't there. Then I recognized it as a show of respect—within the same family. Imagine that.

So far, this has been little help on how and when to switch from *Pan/Pani* to first names. Here's the most precise answer I could cull from Poles: It's based on feeling, relationship and atmosphere. In other words, it's not always clear to them either. In the case of uncertainty or unequal status, it's safer to wait for the other person to suggest, *Przejdźmy na Ty* (Let's move to Ty) Or, if appropriate, suggest it yourself.

Americans usually relate to each other on a first name basis except in the case of great age or power differences. People will correct you immediately if you're being too formal by using Mr., Ms., Mrs., Dr., or Your Honor. Or, if after a long time, Mr. Espino says one day, "Oh, listen, just call me Nate," there's an uncomfortable adjustment period when you avoid calling him anything. Tentatively, you manage to say "Nate."

I had an experience like this with a professor who, over the years, has become a friend as well as a mentor. He's always been "Dr. Harris" to me, the appropriate address for a professor-student relationship. He first signed his letters and postcards with his initials, DPH, then with his name, Dave Harris, then most recently, just "Dave." I can't very well write him back and address him with a blank. I think I'll write, "Dear Dave, You owe me a *Bruderszaft*."

ⓢ Dubbing Rights

Remember the hackneyed retort to someone calling out your name? "That's my name! Don't wear it out!" Well, the risk of wearing out someone's name in Poland is lower than in the States. There are oodles of nicknames for friends and loved ones in Polish.

Nicknames are typically signs of intimacy, affection and solidarity. In Polish, one way to form an affectionate name is with diminutive suffixes. *Piotr* for example might be called *Piotruś*—something like "Petey." A last name might be shortened, like Fiłonowicz to *Filo* or *Jajkowska* to *Jajko* ("egg").

Another way Poles show affection is by using pet names—literally—since they come from animals. Animal names for lovers, close friends and children are not common in English (though I will confess that my dad used to call me Lambie-pie when I was a kid). In Polish, *Koteczku, Żabko, Ptaszku* and *Misiu* (Kitty, Froggie, Birdie, and Little Bear) are typical. One Pole says her favorite way to refer to loved ones is *Misiu Puszysty,* which means something like Fuzzy Little Bear. Ain't that sweet? It's even cute to call someone *Rybko* (Fishy) which sounds much more romantic in Polish than English.

In intimate relationships, you have the dubbing rights to terms of endearment (like Sweetie or Poopsie). In Polish, *Skarbeczku* is Little

Treasure, and *Mała* (Little One) is very popular for little girls or even girlfriends. *Kochanie* means Lover, and *Kochany* or *Kochana* is Dear, which you might even hear from friendly folks (especially older women) who work in shops or restaurants.

Then there are nicknames that just stay with people from childhood or schooldays. For instance, a man whose last name is *Zbojnicki* is called *Zbój* (Bandit) to this day. Other nicknames might come from physical or personality traits. One Pole has always been a little thin on top so his name is *Łysy* (Baldy). Another guy's nickname was *Niuniek* (something like Junior) since he always acted like such a kid. Finally, in his thirties, he told people to quit calling him that even though his behavior hasn't changed much.

People who use each other's nicknames identify themselves as members of a certain group; it's a sign of solidarity. Traditionally, men are more inclined to make up and use nicknames than are women. They also use friendly, informal terms of address more often. Sometimes Polish men call each other *stary* (old one), *chłopak* (boy) *or facet* (guy) as in *Cześć facet* (Hi, guy).

Of course, there are some nicknames people would rather just forget. A Pole was surprised to hear that an old high school buddy had been appointed a high ranking government official. "*Morda?!*" (Animal face?!) he said in disbelief.

The Polglish Language

"I have *małe pytanie*," an American says to a Polish co-worker. "*Muszę wziąć ten* ticket," a Pole travel agent tells her Polish colleague. "Sorry," a Polish soccer player calls out to his Polish teammate after missing a pass. "*Było* super," a Pole says about an event.

Boże! I mean, God! What's wrong with these people? Can't they keep their languages straight? Nope. And there's nothing wrong with them either. Like it or not, combining languages is a natural phenomenon. There are even names for the ways speakers create hybrid communication by cross-breeding languages: code-switching, code-mixing, and borrowing.

The most obvious of these processes is "code-switching": Bilinguals change languages according to conversational partners, situation, or even topics within the same conversation.

"Code-mixing" means including single words or phrases from one language while speaking another. Purists turn their noses up at this common process and sneer at "Franglais" or "Spanglish." Many speakers of Polish and English use what I guess we should call "Polglish."

For example, a Pole said to me "My wife is *bardzo* right." My Canadian friend's knee-jerk response to my suggestion for another round of beers is always *dobrze*. A Polish-English bilingual kid begged her bilingual uncle, "Can we go to the *sklep teraz*?" Some Americans have adopted the Polish clipping of *dziękuję* to *dzięki* into English and even nativized it to *dzienks* to make it sound like "thanks."

There are patterns to code-mixing; for example, people tend to code-mix key words that are oft repeated. But the mixture can also be highly individual, unpredictable and obscure. Exactly for this reason, it is particularly fascinating to linguists—that's the wacky world of academics for you.

Often foreign words are used in another language if they represent a concept for which there is no exact equivalent. Polish employees at a large American organization often say, *Idziemy na lunch* and then grab a quick sandwich for a mid-day break. The Polish word for the mid-day meal *obiad* is something else—a longer sit, preferably at home, a bit later in the day.

There is also *drugie śniadanie* (second breakfast) which is a late-morning snack, but it's still not quite "lunch." "Lunch," by the way has great "borrowing" potential: a word permanently adopted from a foreign language and universally recognized by native speakers (the term is really a misnomer; speakers never borrow and then give a word back later when they're done with it). Sometimes, a word's appeal as a borrowing defies explanation. For some reason, the English word "weekend" has become a borrowing in many languages, including Polish.

Borrowings from business English have recently inundated the Polish language, especially in multinational corporations. Companies have a *dział marketingu* and if you have problems, you can *dzwonić do helpdesku*. Your colleague might request information by saying *rób mi update, rób mi briefing* or *daj mi feedbacku*, or complain about *kiepskie deadline'y* (or *dedlayny* if you prefer the hyperpolonized version).

University of Warsaw linguist Jan Wawrzyniak notes how the borrowing of the word "manager" (*menedżer*) into Polish has replaced the former Polish equivalent *kierownik*. *Menedżer* in Polish means a highly responsible, dynamic type. This person enjoys much more prestige than a *kierownik* who supervises only a few people and who now represents, in the brilliant words of Wawrzyniak, "just a poor fart."

⑨ Favorite False Friends

After my first few weeks in Poland, I trundled merrily down to the *Landrynka* to do my laundry. Much to my disappointment, it was just a shop full of sweets; *landrynka* means candy. I felt pretty stupid, but it's experiences like that which really drive home new vocabulary. I had haplessly fallen victim to what I thought was a cognate.

Cognates are words that look alike in two languages, share the same root, and have similar meanings. Such words can be a real boon to the morale when struggling with a new language. But there are also words that look very much the same and have very different meanings. Such pairs are called false cognates, false friends or *faux amis*.

One harmless false cognate in Polish is *sympatyczny* which means "nice" rather than sympathetic. This certainly would not jeopardize understanding. The more interesting false cognates are the ridiculous and dangerous ones.

For example, if a Pole says he will arrive *ewentualnie* one evening, it does not mean eventually as in inevitably. It means only "possibly" or "maybe," so don't bake a cake. Conversely, Polish learners of English are amused by the statement, "The doctor's patient eventually died."

On the same note, there's the Polish affirmative *no*, which stands for "yes" (a shortened version of *no tak* for "well, yes"). The "Just Say No" anti-drug campaign would have been a big flop in Poland.

Beware also of the Polish word *karawan*. If you and a group of friends are going to a summer home in the country, do not suggest making the trip in a *karawan;* it could mean "hearse." Traveling with dead bodies can put a real damper on vacations.

Here's a false cognate that could have life-long ramifications for carefree young folk who don't pay attention. A *prezerwatywa* is not a preservative used to extend the shelf-life of foods; it's a condom. If your partner asks if you have a *prezerwatywa*, he or she ain't talkin' about snack foods.

Most people know this semi-false cognate: *Futbol* means soccer and not bubble-headed lardy lugs in plastic armor body-slamming each other for three seconds at a time. That is what we call "American football." The sign *windy* in an office building doesn't mean that the building has excellent air-circulation. It just means there are elevators.

This one confused me on a resume under the heading "education": The job applicant listed his graduation from a *gimnazjum*. I asked him if that meant he was good in sports and discovered that *gimnazjum* is a pre-war word brought back into use for high school or secondary school. It did strike me as odd to think that he had earned a diploma in sit-ups and toe-touches.

If you want to *impregnować* your footwear, it does not mean you want to have intercourse with your shoes. That's sick. It just means you want to waterproof them. On the flip side, Poles would find it equally perverse to hear that somebody waterproofed several of his girlfriends. If you get hold of a box of Black Cat matches, you'll see the matches are impregnated.

Such false cognates can create confusion. If you find yourself in a ludicrous situation, such as trying to convince the *landrynka* candy store clerk to wash your dirty clothes, it's time to buy a good dictionary. Or maybe a washing machine.

ⓢ Crash! Bam! Pow!

Language is arbitrary. When you think about it, our words have no real connection to the things we talk about. Consider the word "dog": There is no inherent relationship between d-o-g and the four-legged animal that goes "woof-woof." If all English speakers in the world called an urgent meeting and voted en masse that from now on, all furry barkers should be referred to as "griflibs," it wouldn't change the nature of the dog. He would still shed on the furniture and slobber on guests. The new word, "griflib," would only change our spoken reference to the critter.

Another example of how words are arbitrary is that in English we say "dog," and in Polish we say *pies*. Big deal, right? You say "potayto," I say "potahto." Doesn't mean we have to call the whole thing off. Consider many familiar "signs." There is nothing in the traffic light's color green which is closely connected to "go." Blue would serve the purpose just fine as long as everybody recognized it as a sign to "floor it."

There are some limited parts of language which are not totally arbitrary. Some symbols for example—the skull and crossbones on poison labels certainly looks like death. And then there is onomatopoeia: sound symbolism—words we use to represent or imitate the sounds we hear. For instance, "buzz" or "murmur" recreates the sound we are describing. In Polish, *drzeć* means to tear and *mlaskać* means "to make smacking noises while eating."

Less obvious is the effect of certain sounds, like the "k" sound in crack, crunch and crinkle. It's easy to hear the role of the "s" sound in some Polish and English words: *śliski* which means slippery; *plusk* for a splash and *swist*—a whistling sound. In Jabberwocky, Lewis Carroll created a creepy atmosphere by creating creepy sounding words: "Twas brillig, and the slithy toves..." Translations of the poem's nonsense words into foreign languages even retained some of the same sounds for a similar effect, since a few sound symbols seem to correspond across languages. And some languages, like Japanese and Korean, make much greater use of onomatopoeic words than others.

Here's an area in linguistic contrastive analysis that even a grandmother could love: onomatopoeic animal sounds. The sound symbols may differ but you can "hear" the sense of the word. And notice the use of word "reduplication" like a dog's woof-woof, ruff-ruff and even bow-wow. In Polish, dogs go *hau-hau* (pronounced how-how). In Polish pigs go, *chrum-chrum* (pronounced hroom-hroom) or *kwik-kwik* (pronunciation: kveek-kveek) and English, oink-oink, none of which renders a good auditory result. Apparently it's difficult to represent a good snort in a word, though I'm open to suggestions. The Polish bird sounds, on the other hand, are especially pleasing. A chick's peep-peep is *pi-pi* (pronounced pee-pee) and the equivalent of tweet-tweet is *ćwir-ćwir* (pronounced something like chfeer).

Isn't that amazing?

But let's get serious here. A sneeze is represented as achoo in English and in Polish, *apsik* (pronounced apsheek). The bang-bang of a gun in Polish is *bach-bach* (pronounced something like bock) or *pif-paf* (pronounced peef-paf) and a grinding noise is *zgrzyt* (pronounced like zgzhit). Knock-knock in Polish is *puk-puk*. For the full effect, ask a Pole to pronounce *brzdąk* (from the verb *brzdąkać*) for those violent strokes on a guitar rock stars are so fond of. To which both Poles and Americans can say, "Shhhhhh!" No analysis needed there.

⑨ When Slang Don't Clang

Language purists, who sniff and purse their lips at anything vaguely improper, condemn slang as if it were limited to uneducated slobs, ex-cons and other undesirables. You know, the types who would clang their spoon in their cup when they stir their tea.

But slang has a tricky way of sneaking into our everyday speech and even winning us over. And that's okay. In a linguist's view, slang has a perfectly legitimate place in the language. But like any level of talk, you just have to know when to use it.

There's always a social punishment for using language inappropriate for the situation. The person who gives a business presentation in informal language ("Okay, you guys, I got this, like, really cool proposal. You're gonna flip...") would fall from the corporate ladder pretty fast. And professional jargon has its own place. Imagine the lawyer who hands a gift to a friend with, "I hereby irrevocably give, bestow and deliver to John Kubiniec all of my rights, title and interest in the following described property—a pencil holder." John would file charges against the guy for improper birthday behavior.

Worship as you choose, but big words aren't intrinsically better than small ones. For example, "Men—it's an insurmountable endeavor to habitate with them yet it's not feasible to terminate their life cycle with a lead projectile" just doesn't relay the same sentiment as "Men—can't live with 'em, can't shoot 'em."

So we speak informally when it's appropriate and those are the times we depend on slang—for several reasons. Mainly, it identifies the speaker as an in-group member, i.e. someone who's, ahem, *cool*. The younger set revels in slang for they need that in-group identity; the older set doesn't worry about being in the groove so they use less of it. Linguist Eric Partrige identified several more functions of slang: "as an exercise in wit or ingenuity, to enrich the language, to reduce seriousness, to induce intimacy, and to exclude others." Besides, there's just some kind of innate tendency to be creative with language.

The nature of slang (and a problem with learning it in a foreign language) is that it changes quickly and varies from group to group.

But sometimes, it worms itself into everyday speech to the point where it's difficult to distinguish slang from the very informal. "Munchies," "neat!" and "to pig out," once limited to the college dorm, have now found their way into the parlor.

You know what this is all coming to.

Let's look at a few common examples in Polish— some slang, some hyper-colloquial phrases—so you can them toss around in informal conversation: Money in Polish slang is *szmal or forsa* like Americans use bucks. There's also *sałata* (salad) and American dollars specifically are *zielone* (greens). Your cut of a deal is *dola* and if it's for something illegal, you might end up *w kiciu*—in the slammer.

A crummy journalist or a hack is a *pismak,* a doctor or a quack is a *konował* (a veterinarian) and a cop, a *gliniarz*. A lawyer is a *papuga* (a parrot). A jerk or a loser who thinks he's great is a *cienki Bolek*. Your basic bonehead, dolt or lug is a *buc*. A little squirt or a punk is a *małolat* and a little brat is a *bachorek* (a little bastard).

A regular old bar or restaurant is a *knajpa* and a hole-in-the-wall or a dive is a *speluna;* for a crummy hangout, you might hear *melina* (where vodka used to be sold illegally). A cigarette or a butt is a *pet* and from prison slang, there's *szlug. Numerek* (a little number) is a cute word for sex, like hanky-panky, and logically, a *szybki numerek* (a fast little number) is a quickie.

Ciuchy is for clothing (like threads or duds) and *gaduła* for chatterbox—these words walk the fine line between slang and informal. If you are a *gaduła*, you probably talk about *bzdety* (nothing, as in meaningless blabber). In the hospital, the injection that makes you woozy before you go under is a *głupi-Jasio* (stupid Johnny). The bathroom or the W.C. is *kibel* (*kibelek* if you prefer the cuter version). When something is *do dupy*, it's like saying "it sucks" but you can criticize or complain about something by using the milder *cienko jest* (it's thin).

These words are all slangy and informal and you can only use them in the appropriate situation. If you test them out during a conversation and are met with sniffs and pursed lips, you judged wrong. Just keep quiet and try not to clang your spoon in your cup when you stir your tea.

🌀 P is for Prefix

One of the amazing things about the Polish language is that you can stick prefixes onto nearly everything. Except furniture. You can add them to one vulgar word in particular and create a whole bunch of completely different (but still rude) verbs. This type of language is useful to know, if only to recognize it's being used in your presence.

First, look at Polish prefixes of which there are boatloads: *od-*, *prze-*, *przy-*, *na-*, *po-*, *za-*, etc. (the list is long). You can take a verb like *jechać* (to go, to drive) and glue on some prefixes and wind up with different words: *przyjechać* (to arrive) or *odjechać* (to leave). Consider this extensive system of prefixation as economic linguistic recycling.

One particular Polish word has prefixation possibilities galore. It's vulgar but we're all adults so let's treat this clinically. The Polish verb *pierdolić* (to fuck) has super-semantic flexibility. It's also considered more vulgar than its English equivalent which has a few recycling capabilities too. For example, the English f-word is an interjection but also a verb. The -ing or -ed forms are used as adjectives. Prepositional particles render different meanings like "fucked up" or "fucked over." Yes, terribly coarse and downright offensive but the point is that we can squeeze several uses out of different forms of one word (for a less offensive example, check out the verb "to put" in the dictionary).

But we don't add prefixes to the f-word so actually the Polish p-word makes the English f-word look pretty sorry when it comes to different forms and meanings. For example, add the prefix *w-* to the Polish form for *wpierdolić* (*komuś*), which means to beat someone up. But *wpierdolić* can also mean to scarf something as in chowing down. Substitute the prefix *za-* and you've got *zapierdolić* which means to steal something. *Podpierdolić* also means to steal, or to report on someone in a nasty backstabbing way.

And then there's *na-*: add that to the Polish p-word and it has the sense of filling up or putting in too much of something. For example, if a waiter serves you a cutlet the size of bean and a mountain of potatoes, he *"napierdolił ci ziemniaków."* That is, he screwed you over with potatoes—the proportions just aren't right. If someone *"napierdolił mi farmazonów,"* it means he's telling me all kinds of lies, filling me up with unlikely impossible stories (*farmazony* is slang for "stories" in the sense that they're not true).

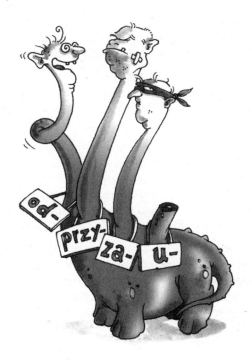

And then this vulgar word can be used like the very ordinary English verb "to put." "*Pierdolnij mi to na stół*" would be like saying, "Fuckin' put that here on the table for me." Here's my favorite: "*Pierdolnąć obrazek na ścianę*" would be "to hang a picture on the wall"—in less than *casual* terms, that is.

Your reaction might be, "Gosh, I certainly don't want to learn to speak Polish like that." Well, I don't either but I do want to recognize what kind of language I hear in the streets or in movies.

The point here is that these little prefixes extend the vulgarity to an amazingly wide variety of meanings. In the language clinic, we appreciate even the dark side of linguistics.

171

⑨ Accent on Charm

People often find foreign accents charming or sexy. Folks are also impressed by foreigners who speak without an accent—that is, without pronunciation errors. That's all a foreign accent is: little errors, which are not a linguistic crime but a natural thing.

Accent also refers to legitimate pronunciation differences, like the typical Boston accent in which the "r" sound after vowels gets dropped: "I pahked my cah." Or some variations are listed in the dictionary like "ee-ther" or "I-ther" for "either."

Accents of all kinds have an affect on people. In an experiment in Britain, announcements were made in a theater requesting people to fill out a survey. When the announcement was made in received pronunciation (RP, standard British pronunciation also known as "BBC English"), more people filled out the survey and gave longer answers than when it was in a nonstandard accent.

When learning a foreign language you think, "I want a perfect accent. It sounds so much better." You tie your tongue in knots repeating a word but someone corrects you. Confused, you protest, "That's what I SAID!" But, it's not. You reproduced the sound in the phonological system that you know. For example, in Polish there's a fine difference between the "ś" and "sz" sounds. The "ś" sounds like the English "sh" but the "sz" is made with the tongue pulled slightly back—a little difference that doesn't exist in the English sound system. It never ceases to frustrate me.

One source of a typical Polish accent in English has to do with the fine distinction between "buck" and "bug." The only difference between the "k" and "g" sounds is that the "g" sound uses some throat action, a vibration of the vocal chords called "voicing." Poles tend to devoice sounds at the end of words. That's why Poles say "Stink" when talking about the musician Sting. And that's why my Polish husband referred to the movie "Silence of the Lamps." I knew he wasn't talking about a horror movie about electrical failure.

So in context, a foreign accent, when not extreme, doesn't usually interfere too much with communication. For example, most non-native speakers of English find it clumsy to place the tongue between the teeth to make the "th" sound. "Thirty-three" comes out as "turdy tree" or "think" as "tink" or even "fink." But who would misinterpret these words in context?

Don't feel sheepish if you speak with an accent; it's part of your identity. An American who spoke Polish as a boy over 40 years ago retained his impeccable pronunciation. But now he speaks limited Polish. When he produces flawless short sentences, taxi drivers and shop clerks rattle on to him as if he's Polish. But he doesn't understand. He wonders if they think he's just a big bonehead.

To improve your accent, have a drink. In an experiment on pronunciation, subjects who drank one and a half ounces of alcohol performed better on a Thai pronunciation test than those who drank the placebo. Naturally there's a limit: Those who consumed two to three ounces of alcohol did worse than the alcohol-free group. (The researcher tried a similar experiment with Valium—it didn't seem to affect pronunciation at all. Maybe people just felt better about taking the test.)

In the worst case, a foreign accent can interfere with communication. In the best case, people like it. So don't worry too much about your accent—it's rare when others find our errors enchanting.

⑨ Starting to Get It

Some people flourish in cross-cultural relationships, but others flounder, fight or withdraw. Finding your footing among people from other cultures means behaving naturally...eventually. The ride might be rocky, but having the right personality characteristics and behaviors helps to smooth the road.

As an American who has lived in Poland for 10 years, I've run the gamut with Poles. I've confused, offended and enraged them. I've also entertained, charmed and engaged them. I've even forged some deep friendships, mainly by behaving naturally, but not without making some essential adjustments. Watching other expatriates do the same is often entertaining and sometimes painful, but the process teaches us a lot about cross-cultural communication.

Here I identify four personality characteristics that are key to successful cross-cultural relationships. In addition to my short list here, there are, of course, other personality traits or behaviors that are essential to successful cross-cultural contact (tolerance of differences, open-mindedness, empathy), but for now let's deal with four of less obvious ones: go-with-the-flow attitude, a flexible ego, risk-taking, and an ability to laugh at yourself.

All four have links to behaviors observed among successful language learners. Of course, speaking the language of your "target culture" helps, but this is not always possible or practical, especially if the language is "difficult." (By the way, there are no inherently "difficult" languages. It's only difficult for *you* if the language is far outside your own family of languages).

These four personality traits and behaviors don't guarantee success, but they certainly lubricate the process of fitting in with people of other cultures:

Go-with-the-flow attitude

An American management executive was posted to Poland, and my task was to help him and his wife learn about Polish culture soon after they arrived. One of the things I did was to arrange a traditional

Sunday *obiad* (afternoon meal) with my Polish in-laws in their typically small apartment. His wife delighted in the experience, chatting with the hosts, admiring their artwork. He, on the other hand, struggled to understand what exactly "obiad" was (Who usually attends? How many people? Just family, or friends too?). Before the meal began, he asked what the menu included in order to plan his eating. He didn't want to fill up on one dish only to find another one served for which he would be too full...and would there be dessert, too?

While his intense curiosity seemed to amuse my in-laws (go-with-the-flow types), his desire to understand the details distracted him from the whole point of the visit.

Another way to look at "go with the flow" is through the psychological functions of the Myers-Briggs Type Indicator (MBTI), Perceiving vs. Judging: People who prefer the Perceiving function enjoy experiencing just how things are, gathering information and being spontaneous. Judgers, by contrast, feel more comfortable with plans, order and control, and making decisions. Judgers may be more effective in accomplishing things, but Perceivers are better candidates for cross-cultural understanding; they're just along for the ride. During our dinner, the wife behaved like a Perceiver, the husband like a Judger.

We can also observe how successful language learners go with the flow, demonstrating a high tolerance of ambiguity. That is, delayed comprehension doesn't cause them great anxiety or discomfort. They're happy to understand the gist and don't have a compelling need for word-for-word or line-by-line translations. They figure they'll "get it" eventually.

The wife "got it," but the husband didn't—he spent so much effort searching for line-by-line explanations, the whole cultural experience escaped him. My sister-in-law later said he behaved as if he were in a difficult situation. Through the company grapevine, I later heard that, indeed, he did have a hard time in Poland.

Risk-taking

A Canadian banking consultant stood up to make a presentation to an audience of 100 Polish bankers, many of whom didn't speak English. He started his speech in Polish—faulty Polish, full of pronunciation errors and grammar mistakes (a polite description). He welcomed the guests and introduced himself and his role in the bank project. The audience almost managed not to laugh. Then the Canadian stammered through a story about how he was dropped on his head as an infant and how the doctor gave his mother the bad news: He would wind up as a banker and never speak Polish well. The audience loved it.

Once he earned their acceptance, he continued on in English with the help of an interpreter (true to his banker nature, he mitigated the risk).

He took a professional risk by exposing his language weaknesses before his peers. After airing his dirty language laundry, he cracked a joke about bankers—another risk. And starting a public presentation with a joke is also risky—if it bombs, you feel stupid.

Again, look at the characteristics of successful language learners. Risk-takers will guess, make errors, sometimes to the point of looking foolish or playing the clown. That is, they'll say something, anything, despite grammar, vocabulary or pronunciation errors, because they're motivated to communicate. Good educators in all areas know that the best learners advance by learning from mistakes, not avoiding them, and then trying again.

Language matters aside, fitting in with people of other cultures necessitates risk-taking and mistake-making. We *are* different, so misunderstandings, mishaps, even disasters, are inevitable. The chances of building cross-cultural relationships without error is zero. Risk-takers treat mistakes as a natural part of the game: They learn and just keep playing.

People will often forgive your errors, but if you get an unexpected reaction, like silence or anger, it's a good idea to apologize, ask if you've done or said something wrong—again, a risky thing to do.

There is always the unfortunate possibility that you'll come across people who won't understand or forgive your errant behavior . Salesmen, actors and writers accept rejection as a professional hazard. In building cross-cultural communications, it's also part of the job.

A flexible ego

Many (many) years ago, a friend of mine in the U.S. went to Austria to study German as part of her university studies, while I went to France to study French. Later, we got together and found we had similar experiences but opposite reactions. I barely understood my French university classes, often felt uncomfortable in my everyday interactions, and made only a few French friends—mainly ones who seemed to take pity on me. But overall, I found the experience challenging and stimulating. My dear old friend also felt lost and alienated in Austria, and she despised the experience of being a child in language, an adult in thought. She felt like a social clod even when socializing in English and made no friends. Her down-graded social status was just too much to bear and she swore off foreign studies. Her ego just couldn't adjust.

Let's look again at language acquisition studies: Ego-permeability refers to a learner's ability to take on a new identity as they increase their competence. One theory states that this is why children learn accents in other languages quickly: Their boundaries of language ego are still very flexible.

Now extend this concept to interacting in a new culture. During the process of adjustment, you have to be willing to develop another identity by absorbing the new rules of how to behave and how to express yourself. And this involves conflicts. For example, extroverts (especially dominant ones) need to shut up, observe and operate from a "one-down" position. Introverts might need to struggle even more to get heard. But, if you have a flexible ego you can deal with the conflict, adjust, build a comfortable identity that fits in with the culture, and still remain true to yourself.

And that's the trick of cross-cultural communications—adjusting your identity and behaviors to the people and culture around you without abandoning your own self. This leads to deeper relationships and true cross-cultural exchanges. Otherwise you're just a chameleon, changing your persona to fit in with whomever you happen to be with that day—a superficial existence.

The ability to laugh at yourself

Some Indian friends and I were dining out at a Polish restaurant. My Indian friend laid her knife and fork next to each other on the side of the plate, the signal that she had finished eating. So the waiter tried to remove her plate. She protested. She ate some more and then returned her knife and fork to the same position. Again the waiter tried to take the plate. She protested loudly, waved him off and condemned the service. I explained the signal she had inadvertently given, but I'm not sure it registered. She was too irritated.

This would have been a good time for her to laugh at herself, but that wasn't her style. Humor doesn't always translate in cross-cultural situations, but lighthearted self-deprecation usually comes across well. It involves risk-taking, as it can highlight a weakness or a mistake, but so what? We already know that mistakes are natural. Revealing a weakness is not only a very human thing to do; it also creates intimacy.

As I was getting to know my Indian friend in Warsaw, I sometimes teased her (my own risky behavior), but she put a stop to that early in our friendship, as she took her personal shortcomings seriously. I refrained from teasing (adjusting my identity to her), and we became good friends. Now living in the U.S., she is pursuing a degree in computer animation. When we chat by phone or e-mail, she describes funny situations of an Indian adult woman trying to find her way among American-kid colleagues at the university. She's beginning to laugh at herself.

She had bounced around the world, living in Indonesia and England before Poland. She once confessed that she didn't enjoy her initial international experiences, but enjoyed her time in Poland. "I'm starting to get it," she told me. Now she seems to have adjusted well to life in the U.S.

She's a good example of someone who has passed through the process of adjusting to other people and cultures—developing a go-with-the flow approach and ego flexibility, learning to accept risk and to laugh at herself. Of course, there are many more factors to explain her success, but now she's different from the person who got angry at the waiter in the restaurant that night.

Some people, unfortunately, won't ever learn to cope with cross-cultural communication; they may suffer from relationship problems in their own culture. Other people don't have to develop the behaviors I've outlined here: Their personality traits help them form good cross-cultural relationships with little effort. They behave normally with just a bit of tinkering. Others bumble, learn some tough lessons, and eventually develop a natural stride they're comfortable with. I suspect that describes most of us.

Your Final Task

The American Quiz

No matter what the passport says, the following quiz will measure just how American you or your friends are:

1. Does your cooking specialty in any way involve a microwave oven? 1 point for yes; 0 for no; -1 if you never lived in a house with a microwave.

2. Do you know who Sponge Bob Squarepants is? 1 point for yes; 2 points if you're a big fan; -1 if no.

3. Do you feel a civic duty to do some sort of community service? 2 points for yes; 0 for no; -1 if you don't think about it.

4. Does it annoy you when there isn't enough ice in your drink? 1 point for yes; 2 points if you like the glass stuffed with ice; 0 if no.

5. Do you believe in the power of positive thinking? 1 point for yes; 2 points if you think it's a stupid question since the answer is obviously yes; -1 for no.

6. Do you tend to introduce yourself to strangers at gatherings? 1 point for yes; 2 points if you'd reveal personal information; 0 for no.

7. Do you wear a class ring from your college or university? 2 points for yes; 0 if no; -1 if you've never seen one.

8. Have you ever been to brunch at someone's house? 1 point for yes; 2 if you've held one at your house; -1 for no

9. Do you keep your hair well-trimmed? 1 point for yes; -1 if you don't think about it.

10. Do you exercise regularly? 2 points for yes; 1 point if you often say you'd *like to* but don't have the time; -1 for no.

11. Do you have a framed needlepointed message hanging in your house? 1 point for yes; -1 for no.

12. Do you ever chew gum in public? 1 point for yes.

13. Do you own *anything* that has your initials on it? 2 points for yes; 3 points if it's a monogrammed shirt.

14. Have you ever regularly watched a TV show that had a laugh track? 2 points if yes; -1 if you don't know what that is.

15. Do you know how to make Ranch chip dip? Rice Krispie Treats? 1 point for each yes; -1 for each you've never eaten.

16. Have you spent an evening playing board games with friends? 1 point for yes; 2 points if at your house; -1 for never.

17. Is "wow!" or "oh my God!" part of your vocabulary? 1 point for each, 0 for no.

18. Do you like Girl Scout Cookies? 1 point for yes; -1 if you don't know what they are.

19. Would you ever tell a stranger to put out a cigarette? 2 points for yes; 1 point if you'd just shoot the person dirty looks; -1 point if you smoke.

20. Can you drive only an automatic shift car? 1 point for yes.

21. Do you ever slap high fives with people? 1 point for yes; 2 points if often during conversation; -1 if never.

22. Do you tend to refer to the time it takes to drive to a place rather than the distance? 2 point for yes.

23. Do you wear chinos or khakis? 1 point for yes; 2 points if they're L.L. Bean or Eddie Bauer; 1 bonus point if you wear Docksiders too; -2 points if you don't understand any of this.

24. Do you know the basic rules of baseball? 1 point for yes; -1 for no.

25. Do you ever smile at strangers in public areas with no self-interest? 1 point for yes.

26. Do you strongly believe in the principle "The customer is always right?" 1 point for yes.

27. When people ask you "How are you?" do you usually give a positive response? 1 point for yes; -1 if you often tell the unpleasant truth.

28. Do you believe that with hard work and determination, you can rise up and accomplish your dreams against all odds? 2 points for yes.

30 points or more: You're true red, white and blue—the cheese on the burger. Mom, apple pie and Chevrolet. Strong possibility you're a Republican.

20 to 29 points: You're quite American. Maybe a Democrat.

8 to 19 points. If you're a Pole with this score, it's understandable—impressive even. If you're American, you need a trip home. You're starting to slip.

-8 to 7 points: You may walk and talk American, but you're out of it, pal. If you go to the States, better stick to your closest friends and family. Or maybe you're just American enough to tolerate born and bred Americans.

Less than -8: Whoa! You probably think Americans are an exotic, happy people.